IN SEARCH OF GOLD

Captain William John Chads MC

In Search of Gold

Amazing Adventures into Unknown Country on Foot and Horseback

DIANA CHADS

The Pentland Press
Edinburgh – Cambridge – Durham – USA

First published in 2001 by
The Pentland Press Ltd
1 Hutton Close
South Church
Bishop Auckland
Durham

ISBN 1-85821-803-9

Typeset in Adobe Garamond 12/15
by Carnegie Publishing, Carnegie House,
Chatsworth Road, Lancaster

Printed and bound by Antony Rowe, Chippenham, Wiltshire

To Kit and Alma Platt,
with grateful thanks for
their friendship and kindness

Contents

Foreword

Captain Chads came from a family with a long tradition of distinguished service in the Navy and the Army and it was after he had retired from the Army that he spent a number of years travelling extensively; this book deals with his travels in South America, and he also spent periods in Angola and Nigeria. This account of some of his adventures and experiences is based on descriptions in his letters, journals and photographs which fortunately have been preserved. He was obviously a resourceful and capable man who enjoyed exploratory travel in difficult areas, quite apart from any mining business objectives which may have justified his travels.

Captain Chads must also have been highly adaptable, because, by the time I came to know him, his travelling days were over and he had single-handedly been looking after his twin daughters from a very early age and had formed a very close family with them. I knew him as a good-looking, likeable person, who made friends easily and had a great sense of fun. He was a great devotee of opera and ballet and a regular supporter of the Royal Opera House, Covent Garden, and was no doubt responsible for his daughters' great musical interests as well as sharing his enthusiasm with his friends.

This book provides an interesting glimpse at one period in the very varied life of an unusual man.

Kit Platt

Preface

illiam (always known as Captain Chads), was a real English gentleman. He was tall, handsome and always spoke in a friendly and kindly manner.

He was a born explorer and wrote frequent and lengthy letters home about his experiences. All his letters were kept and at a later date he typed out extensive notes about his extraordinary experiences into unknown and dangerous territories. These notes were kept in two ringbinders with the idea of revising them at a later date, but this never happened.

William was a keen photographer and although the pictures of South America and Africa (the subject of another book) are old they give a clear picture of the places visited.

William's father was in the Army and stationed in Brisbane at the time of William's birth. He was born on 13 February 1893 when there were severe floods and his birth took place on a roof top.

The family came home to England and in September 1907, when he was fourteen years old, he entered Cheltondale College, Cheltenham. By the time he was seventeen he was a prefect. William excelled in sports and played hockey, football, rugby and cricket in his house teams, often as captain. He also excelled in fencing, was a good tennis player and enjoyed boxing.

On leaving school he joined the Army and started training at the Royal Military Academy at Woolwich. He was appointed Second Lieutenant, Special Reserve of Officers, at the Cork Royal Garrison Artillery on 10 October 1913, aged twenty. From 11 August 1914 he joined the Land Forces in the Royal Horse and Royal Field Artillery and soon found himself in France during the bitter fighting

of the First World War. He particularly enjoyed serving as aide-de-camp to General Wardrop for whom he had great respect. His work often involved a high degree of bravery, especially when involved in reconnaissance, and this was rewarded on 5 May 1916 when he was awarded the Military Cross.

William was wounded and had to be treated by the medical team, his wounds being such that they had an enduring effect. Having completed a probationary staff course, he was sent to the main staff course with the 58th Division, RFA on 15 October 1918.

Two years after the end of the War travel restrictions were still severe. On 4 September 1920 the British High Commission in Constantinople (Istanbul) issued a document to William permitting him to travel overland via Belgrade to England for one journey only. It requests that 'all Allied Naval Military and other authorities to whom this pass may be presented will afford the bearer all reasonable facilities'. The French issued a pass to travel without stopping via Greece, Bulgaria, Romania, Serbia, Italy, Switzerland and France.

At the commencement of William's travel diary is the following:

WALKING

To the unimaginative, walking is merely the movement by which the legs, in co-ordination with the body, carry a person along because he or she must reach a destination, and walking is the only way this objective can be achieved.

Walking to me and thousands, may be tens of thousands, means striding out for the joy of feeling the muscles respond, the blood flows through the veins with new life, and the thrill of feeling the world to be one's own. Walking creates the 'Merry heart' and so it becomes easier to mount the styles as they appear on the path day by day.

Happily, the walker still exists in modern Britain. Cars and other forms of transport have not yet caused the 'hiker' to give up his own particular way of seeing the countryside. Modern times have,

however, brought pressure to bear upon him. Footpaths disappear, and free access to some beautiful parts of our heritage is placed in jeopardy. It is only by fighting constantly for the re-opening of footpaths and the restoration of ancient rights that the walker goes on with his walking. Yet not all the local bodies and land grabbing individuals can take away the joys which walking gives to those who will sample them. The evening is the most beautiful part of the walking day. On a winter's eve, the lights burn in homely windows, the air naps the fingers, and the tired walker arrives for tea. A warm fire, a pot of scalding tea, and a meal is all he asks. In summer, the church bells ring out as the shadows lengthen across the fields. The feeling of peace is all around and a soft breeze stills the trees as the walker reaches the village or town.

Introduction
Norway – Exploring the Mountains

A year elapsed during which time William had come to terms with the fact that the Army considered his war wounds such that he was unfit for further employment. By now he was becoming restless and wanted more excitement in his life. His first thoughts turned to winter sports in Norway, after which his enthusiasm for travel never ceased.

Friday, 19 November 1921. William had a passport valid for two years enabling him to travel specifically to Norway, Peru, Bolivia, the USA, British Empire, Sweden, Denmark, Holland, Portugal and Portuguese possessions. His visa allowed him to stay until 6 March 1922.

Equipped with the necessary documents William took the boat train from London to Newcastle to board the ship to Kristiania in Norway. The ship departed on time and it was not long before there was an announcement to change the clocks to Norwegian time. William got his belongings sorted out in the cabin and soon dinner was served. Until now everything was busy and exciting but it was not long before William began to think that all was not well with the ship and when he spoke to one of the ship's officers about his concerns he was told that 'it's the worst boat doing the journey across at present.' By 7.30 p.m. William had retired to bed.

Saturday, 20 November. The sea was too rough to do anything but lie still in the cabin.

Sunday, 21 November. William stayed in his cabin all day, only managing to get out of his bunk a few times to look out of the porthole. It did not look as if the sea was really rough compared to a previous voyage he had had, but the ship itself made up for a lot by bumping into a head wind which reduced the speed to 5 knots. For Sunday lunch only three Norwegian captains, an American and a young girl turned up out of a possible forty-five people. On hearing this news William was happy that the company were not making their usual profit from meals.

Monday, 22 November. William managed to get up for lunch but found the food very greasy and uninteresting and all the butter came out of a tin.

Along the Norwegian coastline the mountains were only barely covered with snow. It was a relief to get away from the rough seas and the ship finally arrived at Kristiania twenty-eight hours late. At customs his passport was stamped and the recent snowstorm provided a golden opportunity to enjoy the fun of going from the quay to the Grand Hotel Kristiania by sledge instead of taking a taxi. It was fun to contemplate this mode of transport but in the event it went at a terrifying speed and woe betide anyone who was in the way as they hurtled round the bends; William was happy to arrive in one piece.

William did not have lunch partly to save money and partly to give more daylight time to look round the village. In the evening he had a very good dinner and splashed out on wine. 'I thought my nominal host was going to pay but we shared expenses,' he says. After dinner they went on to a cabaret where, but for a horrible dragon of a chaperon, they would have made the acquaintance of two charming young ladies who looked as if they were French rather than Norwegian. The cabaret show was fairly good, but as they did not understand much Norwegian they left and William went to bed at 11.30 p.m. feeling he was now living in the lap of luxury and comfort, but at a price. At this time of night

the locals normally went on to dancing places where they could find masses of partners! William observed that the girls appeared to be worse than in England in their craze for the light fantastic, but the men were not so inclined to perform. He also found a high proportion of girls appeared to be bandy-legged, but was assured by others that this was not really so.

Wednesday, 24 November. William found an interesting oyster bar for lunch and although the stout was excellent he was disappointed in the oysters. It cost more than William liked and although he learnt a lot he would not be caught out by an expensive lunch like that again. That evening he caught the night train to Trondheim arriving there at 9.00 a.m. next morning, the journey being pleasant and very comfortable. He shared the bunk with one of the Norwegian trade delegates to Russia with whom he had a slight quarrel at first because he wanted the maximum heating on and all the windows closed. William could not stand the heat and could not sleep either, so they came to a satisfactory compromise after which they had an interesting conversation and got on very well.

In the next carriage were two rather strange people. One was the leader of all Norwegian railway troubles. He was young, fat, lazy looking and very self-satisfied, in fact a most pernicious young man. By contrast the other was a poor, lonely but very nice young Frenchman. William was glad to use his French and sat and chatted to him for over two hours, his vocabulary only failing him when he wanted to talk about politics.

Supper was taken at a small wayside station where the food was well cooked. They had a bottle of beer and a plateful of poached eggs, sausages and mashed potatoes. They could eat as much as they were able to in a quarter of an hour for the price of two shillings and four pence each.

William intended to spend the day in Trondheim but was side-tracked into spending the day on the boat where he had lunch and supper, the day's expenses amounting to little over a guinea.

The boat trip to Kristiansund was fairly cheap. It went slowly

along the coast giving ample opportunity to enjoy the beautiful scenery but it was too cold to sit on deck for any length of time.

Thursday, 25 November. On arrival at Kristiansund William checked in at the Grand Hotel. As soon as he got settled in his room he started writing his letter home but soon he had to stop for a short time because he felt a bit sick. The change in weather may have had something to do with it as there had been plenty of frost and snow and now it was pouring with rain all day, washing away the snow that remained and making it all very messy, the temperature being nearly as mild as in England.

Kristiansund was very expensive and on hearing that Finse and Geilo (on the Bergen-Oslo railway) were also expensive he dismissed thoughts of going there. While making enquiries about where to go he heard of a place near Holmerhollen which was well away from civilization and was patronized only by Norwegians. To get there he was told to take the ship to Sindalsören and then drive to a place near Opdal, but if this was too far he could stay at Gjöra for the night. At Opdal he could take the train to Dombas. This sounded ideal and William was hopeful of finding cheap lodgings there.

Friday, 26 November. William got up early to get the boat to Sindalsören. The weather was mild and the boat departed before it was quite light. There was a slight sea mist which soon rose and for a while the scenery was not very great for this part of the world. As they came to the more scenic areas again the fog came down and it was possible to see either the snow-capped peaks above head level or the bottom of the hills. The hills rose most abruptly on either side to a height of between 4,000 and 6,000 feet, and the whole area was covered in snow as the ship moved up the fjord and got further inland. Photography was disappointing because when the light was good the focus was too close, and otherwise mist and fog spoilt the view.

On nearing Sindalsören William heard a ripping sound that was

totally unfamiliar. It was the sound of the ship going fairly fast through the sea which was covered with ice about half an inch thick. They arrived at Sindalsören just after dark. The town consisted of about twenty houses in the centre and about a further twenty scattered in the suburbs which covered a large area. There was one person who spoke broken English. There were electric street lamps and one placed outside each house. The scenery by starlight was lovely and made William feel at peace with the world; the ground was frozen hard as iron and was very slippery.

William booked into the hotel and looking through the register found there had been only three British names in the previous two years. Supper consisted of soup, fish, two chops, potatoes and vegetables finishing with a creamy desert, after which he retired to bed at 9.30 p.m.

Saturday, 27 November. William rose early and soon realized the weather was a bit cold. Breakfast consisted of an egg and much porridge. The total bill was under 10/– (ten shillings or 50 new pence). He tipped them generously because although no-one spoke a word of English they did everything they could to make him feel at home.

Sunday, 28 November. Onward travel to Opdal was a 70 km journey by sledge but it arrived an hour and a half late which was a pity as a good photo was missed because William was unable to stop the sledge in time and then it became too dark for photography. The trip went by frequent short stages, changing from sledges to traps of sorts, according to what the drivers thought fit. The most scenic part of the whole trip was the 10 miles covered at dusk. At one point there was a half-mile stretch of very steep slopes of 3,000 feet on each side of a narrow gully at the bottom of which was a very wild stream. On one side of the road there were icicles hanging down from a height of over 50 feet and higher where they went out of view. Often it was a solid mass of thick ice all joined together. It was quite breathtaking and something to remember,

the beauty of the scenery almost numbing the pain of the bitter cold.

Monday, 29 November. William arrived at Opdal in the morning. It lies at the head of the Sunndals valley and from here he took the goods train for the 75 km to Dombås in order to see the country rather than wait for the comfortable and faster evening train. William, always keen to have fresh air, had the train window open but found it felt cold, although this was nothing to the cold that really hit him when he got out of the train which dropped to 22° of frost. The cold was such that when he put the slide from the camera on the ground for a moment it bent when he tried to pick it up as it had already frozen to the ground.

William booked in at the Dombås Turisthotel and settled there, happy that the bill for travel, two nights hotel accommodation, and two and a half days of food including breakfast, supper and lunch cost a total of only £4.

Things were likely to get more expensive now as William not only

Dombås Hill

wanted to purchase a pair of skis but he also wanted someone to teach him Norwegian. Every time he asked about Norwegian lessons they laughed at him and he soon realized that he would have a rough time if he attempted to speak it; nevertheless he went on looking until he found a teacher.

He was also considering his route home which would probably be by road to Molde and then by boat to Bergen to connect with the ship to Newcastle. Later he changed his plans hoping to avoid Christmas traffic by getting a ship to London.

The air was wonderfully bracing and the Norwegian meals were excellent with plenty to eat, but they always expected him to drink nothing but milk which he found ghastly. Breakfast was a particularly exciting meal with plenty to choose from.

Tuesday, 30 November. William woke up with a heavy cold which he knew was because he was living like he would in England and had forgotten the temperatures were different there. He opened the window of his bedroom when there was 20°F of frost outside, having to struggle to get it open because it had become stuck with

Dombås Hill from hotel

paint. The problem was that being unaccustomed to duvets William felt he had a mattress eighteen inches thick above and below him and he had to kick the top duvet off half a dozen times during the night to get cool again. By morning he was uncovered, freezing cold and felt he had had a very bad night. It was all very annoying. Trying to get rid of his cold was very expensive as whisky and brandy could only be obtained with a medical certificate which again cost money.

Wednesday, 1 December. The cold got worse and in the evening his temperature went up rapidly so he went to bed. Luckily the doctor allowed him some brandy without making a visit and he drank half a bottle in 'hot toddies' (brandy with hot water and sugar). He managed to get blankets instead of the duvet which was much more comfortable.

William then 'trained' the hotel staff to give him an English breakfast, suitable to the climate. He had porridge, cold ham, brown bread, butter and very good marmalade. The cold lasted more than a week and to get clean handkerchieves became a problem because since arriving in Norway he had had great difficulty in getting his washing done, admitting his own attempts were not very successful.

Thursday, 2 December. Still very unwell, William remained in bed living on sloppy food and brandy.

Friday, 3 December. At last he managed to purchase a pair of skis for £2, but without sticks which he borrowed. There was not much snow but sufficient for a beginner and he went on to boast: 'I see no real difficulties before me in the noble art of skiing. It is not very difficult to start and I fancy at no period is there much real skill in it. With a fortnight's practice, with the exception of big jumping, I don't see why one should ever fall.'

Saturday, 4 December. William got a good ski instructor and felt

he was progressing, though he could still touch the bottom of the snow easily with both hands. The instructor told him that it was quite easy to stop quickly anywhere and at any pace to which William agreed, but added that it wasted a lot of time getting up again.

Sunday, 5 December. The skiing here was fun but there was no skating to be had within several miles. William thought ten days in one place was enough and he might go to Finse after all where there was a covered skating rink which was lit at night, and he wanted to try out his specially padded hat.

William used many films while there and sent most of them home to be developed fearing poor results because it was often so cold the shutter would not always operate. It was also difficult to wrap the films up properly because of a paper shortage.

Meals were often late. Lunch was usually at about 3.00 p.m. and supper mostly twenty minutes late. They only had dinner in winter, and said it was not winter yet – they were only just putting on the double windows.

Monday, 6 December. The cold was nearly gone and the handkerchief crisis was over as at last he had got his laundry back.

His skiing was improving but not at the rate he had at first thought – it was disappointing falling more and more often, and having little control over direction. One particular fall was nasty in that he fell backwards onto a ski instead of the snow, so he went on sliding down in this undignified manner until he hit a rock which did not have sufficient snow on it to soften the blow.

Skiing in Norway at this time was largely a kind of long hike when the ski straps would be loosened to allow the heal to lift. Most downhill skiing was done in deep new virgin snow on long skis which were very difficult to manipulate. Pistes were unheard of and so the techniques had to be somewhat different.

William climbed up part of the local mountain but it was too late in the day to see it at its best. When attempting to take some photographs the camera was almost frozen so that the shutters

would not move as a rule. He put the camera on a time exposure with a very small aperture and hoped for the best.

Tuesday, 7 December. William got up at 7.00 a.m. and proceeded to try and climb one of the mountains. He got up as high as he could reasonably hope to go by daybreak and took a couple of photos. He got back to the hotel by 10.30 a.m. and just when he had a wonderful appetite they happened to produce a rotten breakfast, after which he went off skiing on his own as his guide was unwell. It was an encouraging morning with few falls, and places where he usually came to grief he managed to pass safely; to top it all he even managed to get round two bends in the manner intended, but something still told him that jumping would have to wait for another year.

William took the night train to Kristiania having stayed at Dombås Hotel for about nine days. Initially he was put in a third-class sleeping bunk for three people (but hardly big enough for one) and was in his pyjamas when the mistake was discovered. Consequently he had to walk a long way in rather cool air carrying his clothes to the correct compartment. It was worth it as he got a larger compartment to himself instead of a very small one for three people which he would have found quite suffocating. William appreciated his good fortune because the Norwegian trains only had second- and third-class compartments (no first class), and it was not easy to get a bunk to oneself.

Wednesday, 8 December. The train arrived at Kristiania at 6.00 a.m. and William stayed the night at the Victoria Hotel.

The customs at Kristiania would not let William have his pistol back and he had difficulty finding out how to send it to the customs people at Bergen or Newcastle. It took over two hours to sort out, during which time he was taken to eleven offices, some twice, and one even four times.

Thursday, 9 December. William was up early to catch the train to

Finse which was due to leave an hour before dawn. He had to wait for breakfast and then no porter arrived to help get the baggage down to the station, so that by the time he got down there he only caught the train by the skin of his teeth. Finse has the highest hotel and railway station in Norway, situated on the Bergen-Oslo line. The scenery was beautiful and the weather perfect until about two miles from the highest point where every puff of wind that makes the North Sea rough seems to gather and it is quite inconsequential which way it blows. Despite the shock of the cold and deep snow William was advised that 'it hasn't started yet'. Much of the railway line was covered by stretches of long wooden sheds to stop snowdrifts covering the line. The whole area was extremely exposed and wild, giving the feeling that it was the top of the world. There was a team of huskies there which were used for pulling sleighs, the dogs being tethered on long chains and only let free for work.

On arrival at the Finse Hotel the owner said they were closed for painting and were not due to open for another week, although it did not matter as they kindly allowed him to stay as the only guest, giving him a very good room. He took his daughters to Finse in the summer of 1947, twenty-six years later; again the hotel was closed but they had no hesitation in allowing them to stay as long as they wished. We have always been impressed with the kindness of the Norwegian people who go out of their way to help visitors enjoy their country.

William wasted no time in getting to the indoor ice rink where he spent an hour and a half of agony skating. The skates were a bit too small and he only had one pair of boots which he reserved for skiing, commenting 'shoes do not support a great deal'. It was his first time on ice and to start with he could not move. He did not know what to do and it felt so hard underfoot. Then when he did get started in rather a feeble way he foolishly started to rag with some small children. Some of them were marvellous skaters and never fell. They immediately challenged him to catch them but this only added to his problems.

Holmenhollen (nr Oslo)

Skating rink at Finse

Finse Hotel with Scott memorial

William took stock of his expenses and thoughts of going from Gothenburg to London were dismissed as too expensive, but luckily Bergen-Newcastle was cheaper than the other way round. Money was rapidly running out yet he hoped to get back home by 22 or 23 December without having to work his passage or go to the Consul in Bergen for assistance.

Friday, 10 December. From 10.00 a.m. until 1.00 p.m William had a good skiing session with many falls and after a break set off again from 2.00 p.m. until 3.30 p.m. during which he met his Waterloo. There was a particular place which William had tried many times to negotiate but always failed. Finally he went at a terrific speed (for him) and got to the bottom still standing on his skis. This feat was the more remarkable because there was a jump which he had not calculated on and to his surprise he landed on his feet. He was so amazed and delighted that he started to laugh but stopped suddenly when some snow hit him in the face and neck, and the skis hit him on the back of the head. After that he had more falls than ever before, but the snow was deeper and so he felt nothing worse than being a bit wet and, although he had left his cardigan behind, he had no trouble in keeping warm. If that was not enough he then finished the day by skating from 4.20 p.m. until 6.50 p.m., so having had a total of seven hours exercise he called it a day.

Saturday, 11 December. It had been raining during the night and now the temperature was nearly 4° above freezing which was astonishing for Finse at this time of year. William awoke a bit later than usual and had breakfast at 9.45 a.m. He then transferred his skates from his shoes to his boots, but found it difficult managing with only one pair of boots for skiing and skating. He skated for two and a half hours in the morning.

Two children aged three and four were climbing up and either rolling each other or jumping down a nine-foot almost perpendicular bank of snow. After this some kind friends put them on

toboggans and whirled them round and round until they flew off backwards onto their heads. The children then howled with laughter and hurried to get back on again for another spill. William was astonished at this treatment and felt sure an English child would not only cry but would die under such treatment and the mother would have a fit. In this case the mother was not at all worried.

Sunday, 12 December. There was only 4° of frost and no more snow had fallen. William spent most of the day skating and sewed some buttons onto his breeches. In the evening the wind became quite strong, blowing from the south-west instead of the north-east. During the night it changed bringing with it some fresh snow.

Monday, 13 December. it was good to have a chance to ski a bit before going to the skating rink. William had received some stockings from home which he wore in the seat of his trousers to make softer landings, and he was in the process of devising some kind of neat elbow cushions to give them effective protection.

William's skating progress was such that he could now blow his nose without stopping, although he had to slow down a bit. The chief difficulty was differentiating between turning round to go backwards and stopping suddenly. The former he thought was done by emulating a windmill while the latter was too unpleasant to dwell on.

More time was spent replacing buttons on his breeches as sometimes they came off with bits of cloth as well and had to be hastily repaired to be respectable.

William got his first lot of photos back which were developed in Kristiania but they were disappointing. Part of the trouble was the cold weather, but the developing was bad and the films were not properly washed.

At the hotel there was a photo of the Prince of Wales which he presented to the hotel manager (with a tie-pin of his feathers) as a memento of his stay.

Fleisher's Hotel, Voss (on railway back to Bergen)

Wednesday, 15 December. The hotel was open to guests now but the first arrivals were not due for a few days and it was expected to be full at Christmas. The weather had been mild and rainy for the last few days and still the forecast for Bergen, Kristiania and Gjeilo was rain.

Skating was coming on well and now he could turn round sometimes and had managed to go backwards round the rink. Later he went out on his skis across the lake where he found there were large patches of sticky snow and ice, and so progress was slow. When he got to his 'Waterloo' field he found it was quite spoilt. He gave it a try but found the snow was too thin at the bottom.

William had continued with his Norwegian lessons and was improving but found the language very difficult, although he had the satisfaction of being able to read the placards in the lavatory.

Tuesday, 21 December. After a further week's winter sports William caught the 6.00 a.m. train to Bergen and after staying the night

there he boarded the Newcastle ship and got home in time for the Christmas celebrations.

On 11 December 1922 he got a new permit for Norway which was valid until 30 April 1923 and on 17 December he arrived at Bergen and took the train to Finse for another winter sports season.

CHAPTER I

South America 1923
Encounter with a Criminal

The next four years were very eventful. Only the more interesting episodes were recorded so the text may appear to be a bit disjointed in places. The long journeys described in South America were not undertaken as joy rides but each had a specific objective.

While William was looking for something interesting and exciting to do he saw an advertisement in the *Morning Post* whereby Mr Archibald B. Ford was looking for suitable people to join him in South America for an adventure and to make money. This sounded very interesting to William so he wrote immediately to make enquiries about the proposed trip.

Friday, 30 January 1923. William met Mr Archibald B. Ford and found his proposal had interested a number of people.

Sunday, 8 February 1923. A public meeting was held with legal representatives present. After the meeting William made every effort to ensure he had suitable references regarding Ford. It appeared he was the finest type of pioneer: clever, ready to take risks and responsibility and of unassailable character. His father and uncle were both millionaires and on the Board of Trade. He was personally recommended by two banks and three consul-generals in London.

After being educated at Harrow he was one of the first to enter

the Air Force at the outbreak of war. Following injuries from a plane crash he worked for Vickers (aircraft manufacturers) as their agent in Canada during the rest of the War. He was born to be a wanderer and his personal letters of introduction to various people at all levels of society in South America were numerous and likely to be of great help in finding work. It all sounded very plausible.

A party of four decided to leave on Saturday, 7 March and if they subsequently found they required extra help they would invite some of the other interested candidates at a later date.

---

20 February 1923. William wasted no time in applying for the necessary permits which were granted without any problems. He had had a long talk with the consul-generals of Peru and Chile, both of whom spoke highly of the scheme and he concluded that all was well, especially as Ford had dined with the Bolivian Consul several times during the previous fortnight. He obtained his Peruvian and Bolivian visas on 2 March and the Chilean one on 5 March 1923. The other three men did not have a Bolivian visa as the Consul-General had been out of town for the last few days prior to sailing. They were all required by regulations to obtain a further visa at the train terminus before leaving for Bolivia which made William think that he need not have gone to the trouble to get his visa in London.

March 1923. A legal agreement was drawn up between Archibald Burch Ford of Little Manor, Burnham, Bucks, William of United Service Club, London, Nugent Pashley Peacock of 223 Gloucester Terrace, London and M. Hodgins of Combe Martin, Devon.

The agreement was for one year in which each of the three partners had to pay Ford £300 for his initial work and expenses, £150 on signing the agreement and £150 ten days after arrival at La Paz, Bolivia. They had to pay £5 into the Anglo South American Bank, Old Broad Street, City to open an account. Messrs L. D. Hewett & Co. were paid £57 per passenger on the ship, and they

also had to take up a joint draft through the South American Bank on the Banco de la Naecon at La Paz for £383.6.8. On arrival they had to open a separate personal account and a trading account. Any partner could leave the partnership with fourteen days' notice.

They were going in search of minerals, and any precious stones or discovery of value was to be credited to the partnership and not solely to the individual partner who made the find.

Sailing to South America

Saturday, 7 March 1923. The party of four sailed from London to Arica on the *Lobos*, a cargo boat on which there were half a dozen other passengers. William shared a cabin with Hodgins who, prior to becoming an invalid, had served with the Indian Army and joined the party by applying in the same way as William did. Ford shared his cabin with Peacock, the son of the founder of Hope Brothers and a schoolfriend of Ford's. He also acted as a personal assistant to Ford when he was in London. Peacock had wasted a lot of money and was broke at the time but managed to borrow enough to join this expedition. He seemed to be a disillusioned man, hard but likely to be a good worker.

Sunday, 8 March. On the second day at sea William discovered that one of the two ladies on board was a married woman and Ford's mistress. With four bachelors on board William and Hodgins decided to make it clear that either the lady had to go at the first opportunity or they would leave the party. After some discussion it was agreed that the girlfriend should be set up in her own business in La Paz and she was not to be seen out of town with any member of the party of four.

The ship called at Le Havre for a few hours, after which they had a smooth and uneventful voyage to Colon which is situated at the entrance to the Panama Canal. As the *Lobos* reached the

Dredging near Culebra Cut, West Indies

View of canal from the ship

Caribbean the nights were hot enough for William to sleep on deck using a chair for a bed.

The ship refuelled at Colon where she stopped for two nights. Ford spoke sufficient Spanish to show the party round the small town. They saw the breakwater at the entrance to the harbour and something of the town itself. They saw the Cristobal riding stables, a dense banana plantation and part of an old French canal.

It only took a day to go through the canal. The weather was wet and it was too hazy to get an impression of the great work involved in creating the canal. The most striking feature was the silence with which everything was done. There was no shouting or fuss, just the occasional whistle being used to denote the moments at which routine orders should be given. After leaving the last locks at the Panama end of the canal, the *Lobos* sailed for

Guayaquil – statue in Long Avenue

Guayaquil in Ecuador, after stopping in the oily calm of the Pacific for a few moments to drop the pilot off.

Friday, 20 March. After twelve days at sea some of the other passengers followed William's example of sleeping on deck, but for greater comfort they brought up their mattresses and bedding and slept under the awning.

Saturday, 21 March. Heavy rain commenced that evening and water saturated the chairs and mattresses the passengers were sleeping on. William was lucky as he had a dry mattress and bedding in his cabin, but the other passengers had nothing dry to sleep on.

Sunday, 22 March. The ship reached Puna at the mouth of the Guayaquil River on Easter Sunday. From a distance it looked a pretty little town but on closer examination through field glasses it appeared much less attractive. The *Lobos* was due to wait several hours here for the tide, but as the pilot had made arrangements for a glorious binge on arrival in Guayaquil he saw no reason to delay his departure, even though the tide had not come in and there was a risk of wrecking the PSNC ship.

Guayaquil was about 30 miles upriver. The estuary was wide but in no way striking. The main river had been swollen by heavy rains and was running very fast through exceedingly dull scenery with few tropical plants. Although the forests were dense there was little animal or bird life to be seen. There were, however, pelicans and crocodiles in plenty, which were normally rarely seen so far upriver.

The ship dropped anchor at about six in the evening but owing to doubts about the possibility of landing no-one went ashore that evening. Soon a very heavy storm broke and after a few minutes it eased into a steady downpour which was such that William had seldom (if ever) seen in England.

After sitting on deck in the heat of the day William was now suffering severely from sunburn and retired to bed at about 7.15

Guaquil river transport

p.m. where he spent a long time rubbing in all kinds of oils to try to ease the pain. At nine o'clock there were sounds of trouble in the next cabin – two passengers had got very tight and were quarrelling. One of the ship's officers came along and managed to calm them down, but half an hour later the fight continued, this time with more intensity. The mother of one of the young men managed to get hold of her son and locked him in her cabin. Things then blazed up even more so William and Hodgins arrived in their night attire (or less) to sort things out. Luckily the First Officer arrived at the same time and took charge of the situation. The second man was trying to break his way into the cabin to beat up the man inside again.

Both men were big, and this time the second one could only be calmed by banging his head on the iron floor and knocking him senseless. He was then put in irons and locked away in a safe place.

Then something happened inside the cabin where the mother and son were. The mother was in hysterics and by the time a

forced entry was made she was desperately trying to climb through the porthole. There was no trouble in getting the sixteen-stone son, late of the Air Force, to clear out, and his mother was calmed down and put to bed.

While the mother was being settled someone actually gave the son some more to drink. He appeared fighting drunk and was promptly knocked out. He soon came back for more and was knocked out again, yet still he rose for more trouble. He had to be knocked out for a third time and this time, like his fellow drunk, he was put in irons and removed to a secluded corner where he was locked up.

One they were both safely locked up the First Officer and the others involved in the affair decided it was time to discuss the events over a quiet drink. The conversation was soon interrupted when the mother had another attack of hysterics but it took longer to calm her this time. She wanted to rescue her son from his imprisonment and it was not until one o'clock that she and the rest settled for the night. The ship was anchored a quarter of a mile from the shore and with the rain keeping the temperature cool and preventing the mosquitoes from coming out it was possible to have a comfortable night.

Monday, 23 April. Soon after breakfast the following morning the party went ashore to explore Guayaquil, arranging to meet for lunch at the Grand Hotel Ritz. It was a sticky, steamy heat after the rain and walking along the streets was hard work, not made any more pleasant by the furore created by William's 'topi' (hat). Everyone was staring at him and while he did not understand their remarks he received many respectful salutes from the local soldiers.

The town had been burnt down some thirty years previously and it still failed to be attractive. The buildings were all made of wood. The cathedral looked impressive until you got close enough to see that it was constructed of corrugated iron and plaster, and it shared a wall with the adjacent cinema which had a highly religious name and a less religious reputation. There were many

plazas, some quite pretty, others not. The shops were designed to be cool and had a semi-Eastern appearance.

There were very few electric trams in the town, most being pulled by mules – the number of mules depending on the energy, fancy and luck of the driver. Sanitation left much to be desired. Some of the streets were very dirty and smelly; others were blocked to traffic by huge tarpaulins stretched out across the road for the cocoa to dry on. After the rain started many of the roads were too bad even for this and nothing could move on them except the mud which was gently oozing downhill.

Lunch might have been worse, and was certainly better than the service in the hotel which could hardly have deteriorated further and certainly did not reflect its name. It cost about three shillings per person, including tips and drinks. After lunch it seemed appropriate to have some iced drinks to keep cool, so they had one, but when they called the waiter to replenish their glasses he was not to be disturbed from his siesta.

The next attempt to keep cool was more successful. The party hired an American car and asked the driver to take them round the town and then into the country. For a short time the road was good but soon the driver had returned to the starting place, saying there were no more roads. Apparently there was only about 3 miles of paved road in the whole country and they had already covered two of those several times! The undiscovered mile was probably in Quito. Motoring was followed by shopping with Ford acting as interpreter. The main purchase was a Panama hat at a price far below that in the Canal Zone and it seemed to be better quality. An attempt to buy some silver produced much haggling, the price was high and only the seller was sure that it really was silver.

In the evening William's party dined back at the Ritz and then had a long wait for the rain to stop to allow them to return to the ship in the dry. At the customs house they found the launch had been put away for the night and all the boatmen had gone to bed, but eventually they found a boatman willing to face the strong current to take them back to the ship. On arrival they found the

mosquitoes had got there first and no-one had any sleep that night. William treated his sunburn again and massaged the oils well into his skin, the smell of which kept the mosquitoes away and he had a reasonably good night.

Tuesday, 24 March. The *Lobos* was due to leave early on Tuesday morning and passengers were not allowed ashore again, however, the pilot was lost and did not appear until nearly midday, nearly four hours late.

On reaching Peruvian waters the authorities insisted the ship had to visit Paita for a day to be thoroughly disinfected. Peru and Ecuador were very hostile towards each other and Peru considered that even her territorial waters would be contaminated by any vessel that had visited Ecuador. The two countries had a long-running land dispute over an area containing some thousands of square miles into which no white man had yet penetrated, but which both countries claimed was essential to their welfare.

William was the only passenger to go ashore and found Paita to be a dirty, miserable place. The smell ashore was appalling and the heat was even worse than at Guayaquil. Paita was dominated by sandy hills and the population was entirely European. In the evening all the passengers were happy to get away to the open sea again.

The next stop was Callao, the port of Lima. Here everyone disembarked except William's party of four. They stayed there for three days and got to know Lima well. The first night they dined at the zoo, the fashionable thing to do, and afterwards drove out to Miraflores, the residential suburb of the town. The wide road reminded William of the Mall, but this was much larger. It was about ten miles long and was divided into two distinct lanes for traffic going to and from Lima. At the side were lanes for slower-moving vehicles. The streets were well lit by arc lamps hanging in the centre of the road where the traffic moved very fast and noisily. Fifty years later I witnessed the speed, noise and volume of the traffic, and was amazed at the incredible state of dilapidation the

vehicles were in, and the manner in which they were held together to keep them on the road.

Ford was busy here with the first lot of his credentials and the party was warmly welcomed by various officials.

Thursday, 9 April. After thirty-three days the party of four arrived at Mollendo. Here they were amazed to be told that the Government of Bolivia had requested Peru and Chile to refuse permission for the party to land but no reason was given. The only reason the party could come up with was Ford's suggestion that he had definitely come between the Bolivian in London and his mistress, and that he had been instrumental in the latter getting married. He led the party to believe the affair was probably done through spite and could easily be overcome. The various amplifications of the story sounded probable and rather creditable as Ford's credentials at home were far too good to be shaken by an episode like this, in spite of the woman with him.

The party was allowed to spend the day ashore at Mollendo. The *Lobos* was anchored out at sea so the men were brought ashore in a rowing boat, but the swell was so great inside the breakwater

Callao, Port of Lima

the boat could not come alongside the wharf so the men were picked up from the boat in a basket hung from a crane. A huge price was charged for the trip and the boatmen proceeded to have a fracas to get even more money. William made a dignified retreat from the argument because when attempting to make friends with a dog he was bitten in the ankle. Although it was painful he was still able to look around.

The coastline was quite pretty with hills dropping down to the bays, while the town itself was little more than a small seaside village situated on the edge of the desert. There was the usual squalor but the party managed to find a clean hotel where they had a good lunch. The hotel was surrounded with palms and tropical plants which contrasted with the barren ground outside the hotel confines.

Many cables were sent to London to find out what the problem was with Ford and in the afternoon they returned to the ship without further arguments with the *fletero* (boatmen).

Tuesday, 14 April. Landing at Arica was done in the usual rowing boat, with the baggage being lowered over the side of the *Lobos* and into the rowing boat by means of a very thin and badly worn bit of rope. The boat did not look big enough to carry all the passengers and their baggage – in fact the operation looked distinctly dangerous – but somehow everything was carried safely ashore in one boat and without being swamped. The boatman was very pleased with the fare he received from which they could only conclude that he was grossly overpaid.

William and Ford immediately went to see the British and Bolivian consuls. The latter knew nothing of the problems and granted a visa (until 5 October 1926) to go to La Paz on the next train – which was next day, so the party collected their luggage and booked in at the Grand Hotel Vergara.

Wednesday, 15 April. Next morning the party heard that the Bolivian Consul had received instructions to cancel their visas on the

*The rowing boat used at Arica to land passengers and baggage
from the* Lobos

grounds that their passports were not in order, and refused to
return them. When the British Consul checked the passports he
found William's to be in order and the only error the others had
was not getting the Bolivian visa in London before the voyage
started, which they needed in addition to one from the consulate
in Arica. William thought the excuse was too lame to be real and
it seemed to be a case of spite and nothing worse. The British
Consul showed him a telegram in which it was stated that Ford
was known to be a dangerous man which William found too absurd
to be true. He then sent many wires to the British Minister in La
Paz asking him to clear the matter up, and asking permission to
allow him (William) to travel to La Paz to discuss the matter with
him and the other people concerned. Finally a reply came which
stated that the case had been referred to the President personally
and he had definitely 'refused to sanction the visit even if he

returned by the first possible train after arrival, and travelled under Police surveillance both ways'.

The only remaining course of action was to go to the British Minister in Santiago and a wire was sent to La Paz asking that all information be sent there. The other members of the party decided to move out to Tacna and have a preliminary look round the country. Hodgins took sufficient money from William to cover reasonable expenses and looked after William's interests while he went south armed with masses of letters of introduction. If William was unsuccessful Hodgins was going to return to London and see what he could do there.

Arica was not an attractive town and the hotel was expensive; the food was poor and the drinks were of doubtful origin; it was dirty and smelly with fleas and mosquitoes in the toilets. Camphor balls placed in William's socks helped to keep some of the pests away, but that did not drown the smell.

A battle was fought here in the Pacific War but more recently there had been an earthquake and the tidal wave that followed carried a ship two miles inland where the locals pointed out its rotting hulk with pride to any passing visitors.

There was also an old Inca graveyard where people were digging up corpses. Hodgins took pleasure in doing this and collected a few pieces of tapestry in excellent preservation; the colours were very bright despite the years during which they had been buried. The sand was littered with human bones and skulls and there were a few complete skeletons. Each corpse had its own round and narrow grave into which it had been dropped in a sitting position after being well-wrapped up in clothing and supplied with sufficient food to last for eternity – allowing for very small appetites in the next world.

The bathing was not good – the Pacific was extremely cold and the waves enormous. Swimming through them to avoid a heavy pounding was difficult as there was a considerable undertow. Giving up the open surf William tried a large pool, but this was no better – a sea-urchin made his acquaintance and left a number of bristles in his hand which became very painful and hard to pull out.

The local hill, the Morro, was forbidden territory because it was the site of both the modern defences and of the old Peruvian fort. The locals took great pride in the old battles, the most noteworthy episode being that the Chileans scored a victory and the Peruvian commander took a toss over the edge of the cliff on horseback. The contending parties were not agreed as to the cause of this fall – some saying that he was too drunk to know any better, others that his horse bolted with a man who was incapable of controlling any horse, or that he galloped over the cliff through fright. The Peruvians maintained he preferred death to capture.

William walked round the Plaza and observed what was going on. Arica church was a beautifully proportioned building which stood at the top of some twenty steps that were about three times the width of the church itself. The children playing in the street were amusing to watch and behaved well. They also found William's hat extraordinary and could not take their eyes off it.

Mummy skeleton and skulls at Inca cemetery

A trip was made to look round Tacna which was situated just a few miles inland. At the railway station they found their transport was a Ford car which had been adapted to move on the railway track. It was like a small hut sitting on the chassis behind the engine. There were other tracks to Tacna but only passable on donkeys or mules. Some fifty years later in the South of Chile I saw a similar Ford car carrying about seven railway workers along the track.

Tacna was a military town – a bit like Aldershot in Hampshire – and was cheaper, cleaner and better than Arica in every way. The cathedral only had walls, two towers and a bell – there being no funds to build a roof or provide interior furnishing.

William had invitations to dine with various people connected with horses or guns who were said to be fine horsemen but their horses were poor and badly cared for, and their harness was filthy.

Ford and Hodgins about to board the Ford car on the railway to Tacna

While William went to Chile the other three members of the party moved out of Tacna to have a preliminary look round the country.

Thursday, 23 April. William left Arica for Santiago on the *Santa Elisa*, an American ship which he disliked intensely, although she was very comfortable, clean, and William had a cabin to himself. The food was excellent and it was tempting to overeat at every meal. However he found the Chinese waiters very irritating and unable to speak a word of English so it was necessary to point to the numbers of the courses or dishes required on the menu. Not knowing what some of the dishes were, and sometimes the wrong one being served, William felt embarrassed that he appeared to have a flagrant disregard for the usual order of courses. The ship was dry, but there were occasional visions of someone who had had too much to drink. Most of the passengers were American whose sole topic of conversation was money and this added to William's distress.

Friday, 24 April. Early next morning the ship stopped at Iquique for a couple of hours. It was a miserable-looking place with mud streets, horse trams and many water carts trying to keep the dust down.

At Antofagasta William was escorted ashore by an elderly American. Although nothing special, William found Antofagasta by far the best coastal town to date – the shops were modern and seemed busy and there was a lot of activity in building and shipping. A great deal of machinery was unloaded into lighters for transport to Bolivia. The work was done very quickly, all hatches being worked at the same time filling lighters on both sides of the ship. As each lighter was filled it was cast off and allowed to drift about until a tug was available, but no time was lost in pulling another lighter in to fill the place of the one cast adrift.

There was a high percentage of breakages, partly due to the heavy swell and mainly because the work was done so speedily.

The work was halted for a time by a flight of birds. These birds lived along the coast in millions and their droppings, known as *guano*, is an important source of wealth as it is sold as fertilizer.

In the ports the seas were alive with fish, and the quantity must have been enormous to supply food for the swarms of predators that hunted them. The seals had driven the fish to the surface and the birds dropped in their thousands from forty to a hundred feet to catch them, never seeming to miss. Frequently the horizon was completely obscured by birds hovering in the air prior to dropping like a burst of shrapnel onto the surface of the water. Divers went in making hardly a ripple, gulls of various types dived less elegantly, while the pelicans disdained any fancy stunts and reached the water in the simplest manner possible, by closing their wings while in flight and dropping more or less beak first. The splash was considerable, but they were as successful as the other birds in collecting a fish at each attempt.

The combined noise of the birds screaming and the seals barking

Plaza des Armes, Antofagasta

was such that it was impossible to maintain a conversation in an ordinary voice or for the ship's officers to make themselves heard when shouting orders. Many birds had eaten until they were too full to fly and when the ship sailed were incapable of moving out of the way, in spite of the siren being sounded repeatedly.

The *Santa Elisa* stopped for an hour in the dark at Coquimbo where the lights looked pretty.

Monday, 27 April. The *Santa Elisa* arrived at Valparaiso in the afternoon, the first ship to disembark passengers at the new wharf inside the mole. Disembarkation procedures had not been thought through, the cargo was landed ashore immediately, but passengers had to leave from the other side of the ship, being rowed to the customs offices, which gave the handling staff ample opportunity for theft. Eventually the port authorities and the shipping companies combined to break through the ring of interested people.

William was pleased to leave this ship. There was insufficient space for proper exercise and now he could get on with sorting out the Ford problem.

Tuesday, 28 April. After spending the night in Valparaiso William caught the early train to Santiago. The porter forgot to give him a call so he had to leave in a hurry without taking a bath or having a cup of coffee. His mood was not improved by the heavy mist which obscured all scenery until nearly 9.30 a.m. when they passed through snow-capped hills and very desolate country, bereft of any grandeur and disappointing to view.

The train was of the American type, comfortable, with a corridor in the centre and a single small compartment at one end for a family. It arrived at Santiago at 11.15 a.m. and William went to the Oddo Hotel which was clean and comfortable but he could only get morning coffee for refreshment. The room cost seven shillings a day and by the evening Santiago seemed to be the cheapest town in South America.

Wednesday, 29 April. After cleaning up William had difficulty in finding the Legation. The Minister was ill so he left the papers with the Secretary and made an appointment for the next day.

That evening William went to the Plaza where a band played nightly. It was the fashionable rendezvous – the men and women formed two crocodiles and walked round and round in opposite directions with much bowing and scraping each time an acquaintance met or remet. The women looked pretty and were expensively dressed, but their faces lacked intelligence. The people were well behaved and far better dressed and more decorous than in most European countries. Even today the women take great pride in how they look and no matter how small the village they still dress well and often get their toenails painted at pedicures.

Thursday, 30 April. The following morning William woke late and was unsuccessful in his attempts to get a bath. He therefore tried to wash himself all over in a basin, which proved difficult. After a good walk round he went back to the Legation where he had a long wait during which a young clerk related various stories about the dangers to be encountered in the town at night, which William considered to be interesting and improbable. Santiago is a city where even today people have to be very careful, especially foreign visitors.

In the afternoon William spent several hours at the Cerro S. Lucia, the most beautiful rock garden he had ever seen. Situated in the middle of the city, it was started by Pedro de Valdivia and finished many years later. Pedro de Valdivia apparently treated the native Indians badly. His chief opponent, Caupolican, was captured and burnt at the stake. His wife arrived at the last moment to slang him for being captured alive, even though he was wounded, and finished by throwing their baby in his face to be burnt with him. Soon after this Pedro was captured and a great dinner was arranged. They thought their account was more or less squared with him when they gave him his final toast to drink – it was

molten gold. The statues of these two men are placed at opposite ends of the rock gardens, the Arucanian chief looking over the city with a bloodthirsty expression, while the *hidalgo* (Spanish gentleman) stood gazing into darker corners.

Saturday, 2 May. William finally got to see the Minister on Saturday who confirmed the accusations against Ford were of the most serious nature and recommended the matter be dealt with from home.

That afternoon he went to the Police sports. Many of the events were novel and the horsemanship was good, though it was also very brutal. The first item was against a long bar fixed rigidly to the ground. A number of horses were ridden with their chests against this, while at a given signal another horseman tried to ride his horse between the first lot of horses and the bar. Sometimes in country districts the horseman would attack and defend their positions using their stirrup-irons.

Next came a form of rodeo in which two horsemen had to separate a selected young bull from a small herd in a pen, without letting any of the others escape. The selected bull was then driven round the arena which was in the form of a circular stockade. At the end of each half circle, and just in front of an exit, there was

Santiago – Cerro San Cristobal

a padded area where the bull had to be checked, turned and driven back to the first exit again, where the operation was repeated and maintained until the judges had seen sufficient of the pair working. The bull would then exit the arena (unhurt). The horses maintained a smart canter throughout, one horse being pressed against the quarter and the other the flank of the bull. This form of rodeo is carried on today, especially at Easter parades and on 18 September, Independence Day, where the festivities usually last almost a week and the contestants are often full of *chicha* (unfermented wine from the new grapes).

The horses had to be able to start and stop abruptly and a young horse when trying to halt would somersault over the bull, the greater the fall the louder the applause from the crowd. They also enjoyed two well-padded clowns fighting a young bull, but worse was their enjoyment of an unbroken colt that was kept at the gallop and every few moments made to fall by the lariat (lasso) round a named hoof. The farmers were extremely skilled at catching animals in this way. The horses were often left wild for long periods of time and were hard to catch, but the moment they were caught they calmed down immediately and could be ridden.

Haute école was a display of sudden starting, halting and turning. The bits used were very severe and could easily break the horse's jaw. Sharp spurs were also used, and although a well-trained horse was treated gently, many were not.

While all this went on inside the arena there was continual dancing of the *cueca* in the booths just outside, a dance where the ladies hold a white handkerchief and dance elegantly in front of their young man.

To improve his Spanish William went to the theatre in the evening, which was due to start at 9.15 p.m. William arrived fifteen minutes late but in time to see the arrival of the first of the orchestra. Fifteen minutes later some more arrived and were surprised at the ironic ovation they received. After a further ten minutes the audience were so restive the show had to start. The intervals were long and the audience got even more restive causing some cuts to

be made. The performance finished just after one o'clock. The soloist was poor and the chorus dreadful but it was a night out and only cost four shillings.

Sunday, 3 May. William took a walk up the Cerro S. Cristobal, a large hill just outside Santiago. Avoiding the roads he took any convenient track and a short way up found he had bullets sizzling round him – he had walked behind the butts of a musketry club that had dispensed with flags to mark the limits of the danger area, and they waited until he was immediately behind the targets before opening fire. At the top of the hill he had his worst and most expensive meal in Chile before returning to Santiago to find he was too late for the races.

Monday, 4 May. William dined with two men from the Anglo-South American Bank. Afterwards they went to the British Club for a game of billiards and then at midnight they decided to show him the nightlife of Santiago. They visited many strange places, some of which were almost respectable. Drink was being consumed and its effects were beginning to be realized so William took some Enos which saved him from even a trifling head next morning.

The evening was brightened for a moment by a Chilean who acted as if he owned the world. William wanted to chuck him out of the building but his companions were horrified, whispering in excited tones that it was *Vincentini*, which meant absolutely nothing to William, whose party was outnumbered by five to four, but the others were lusty fellows and their offensive behaviour asked for trouble. William's companions quietly escorted him (William) out of the building. Next day he heard that this man was the Chilean hope for the world middleweight boxing championship.

Ford wrote a letter on 4 May saying he had not heard anything since William left Arica for Valparaiso. Hodgins meanwhile had left, withdrawing his money and refusing to advance any of the £20 which William had asked him to pay towards the horses they

had taken there. The partnership was dissolved and his solicitors were asked to refund any monies due. Peacock had also left.

Tuesday, 5 May. Apart from these digressions William spent much time at the Legation and by now the Minister was fairly certain that he should have no trouble in clearing himself personally but warned that there could still be a long delay. The Minister could do no more from Chile and the matter now rested between the Bolivian authorities and the British Foreign Office. Business being completed William returned to Arica to report progress.

He took the evening train to Valparaiso to board the *Orita*, the next ship to Arica. It had been another day of celebrations for others who were going home that evening and William joined them for the first part of the route. How the party were collected and put on the train was a mystery for which the bank staff deserved great credit. They claimed to have had a lot of experience of that kind of work and William was the most sober passenger there.

As soon as the passengers were settled William found all his papers, letters of credit, tickets for the train and ship, and money had been taken from his pocket. It looked like the most likely culprit was the conductor on the train who had already assisted by opening his bags to get out his reading material.

William referred first of all to the two older and most sober of his three acquaintances on the train, both American, and they set to work in a despondent mood. They thought the best William could hope for was to save the undrawn portion of his letter of credit if he got to the bank quickly next morning. William then spoke to St Aubin, known as the 'Dook', whom he had met a few times during the day. Dook was always gazing in a carefree manner at an empty glass in his hand, giving the impression of being a crystal-gazer predicting that there was no limit to his capacity for drink. He was carrying over £2,000 in his wallet as he was going to Europe for the first time for many years.

At first he wanted to fight as he thought the accusation was pointed at him, but then he became more helpful. He sent for all

the officials on the train and when they had assembled he made a singularly sober speech to them in bad Spanish, but good enough for them to get the message. He gave orders for the train to stop at the next wayside halt, at which it was not due to stop, as he proposed to telephone the Commandante of Carabineros, the President's brother and two leading members of government. He accepted full responsibility for his actions as he was persona grata with these people, and was going to organize a thorough search of the train and everybody on it. The train was going to be delayed until the money was found, and being State controlled this was possible. There was considerable consternation but five minutes later the pocket book appeared, having been dropped on the floor of a crowded compartment, with the contents intact with the exception of the Chilean currency to the value of about seven pounds. William thanked the Dook and remarked on the good use he made of his highly influential friends, only to learn that he had never met any of them and they had certainly never heard of him.

On arrival at Arica William met Hodgins who had booked his return passage on the *Orita*, the ship William had just arrived on. He returned the loaned money intact and said he had definitely finished with the others.

Ford and Peacock had got permission form the Intendente to go prospecting in the mountains and had quickly taken this opportunity to cross the boarder. They had both written a letter to William, Ford an abrupt one and Peacock apologizing for the dirty way in which circumstances had forced him to act. Curiously he bumped into Mrs N (Ford's mistress) who was travelling second class and was in much distress.

William stayed aboard with a few others until the last possible moment, when about two in the morning most of the disembarking passengers and friends left in the Consul's boat. An old resident, known as Onion, led the way, immaculately dressed in whites, straw hat and with an alcoholic stammer. He omitted to see that the rowing boat had failed to come alongside the ship and stepped

straight into the sea, whereupon the boatman rescued him promptly without adding to his indignity. To give a more nautical appearance, Onion stood up on the seat of the boat while he harangued the boatman whom he blamed for his misfortune. The boatman has a sense of humour, the movement was slight and quick, but just sufficient for Onion to find himself back in the sea. His next appearance was in a more sober mood.

William went back to Tacna at once and while staying there the Chilean Cavalry Regiment were very hospitable and allowed him to use their riding school whenever he liked, and he could choose his own horse. Most days the Colonel's own charger was offered.

William wanted to go into the Cordillera and made several arrangements for mules to take him, but on each occasion they failed to arrive. Eventually he was told that the trip was unpopular with the Intendente who simply said 'tomorrow'. It became obvious that he had to move south where the association with Ford would have less ill effects on his movements.

Field mass at celebration of Battle of Tacna

Eliot and Flint about to board new railway carriage on trial run
Tacna – Arica

In Tacna he had Spanish lessons with a charming lady of forty
(who appeared to have paid a fortune for her beautiful smile), to
prepare him for his proposed trip into the Cordillera – the Andes.

Still trying to resolve the Ford mystery William took the ship
back to Valparaiso and went to Santiago by train to stay at a rest
house at Lonquen. It was kept by an English couple, the shooting
was said to be good, and it seemed a good place to await news
from England. The only others there were three invalid ladies who
had prearranged to shock him – the youngest succeeded, but the
other two, being wives of two important men in Valparaiso, had
to be more careful in what they said. He only saw them in the
evening, devoting the daytime to long walks and shooting, which
proved to be very disappointing.

Getting bored with this he decided on a long tour of the mountains north of Santiago to see if there was any chance of resuming the old project.

CHAPTER II

A 900-mile Ride in the Andes

W hen William mentioned his project of a long ride in the Andes to the north of Santiago everyone thought it was foolish as the place was infested with bandits. He was told to see the Comandante of *Carabineros* (Police) in Santiago to get an escort, and was immediately given a man to follow him to the ends of the earth if necessary. His kindness was largely due to his being an honorary member of the United Service Club when he was Attaché in London.

Thursday, 9 July. This man was to meet William at Colina on 9 July. Final arrangements were made at Lonquen. The heavy baggage was sent to Los Andes by rail as he could not find a suitable baggage horse, although he got a strong and very fat horse to take him the 40 miles to Colina, carrying not only him but forty pounds in the saddlebags also.

The route took him directly through Santiago where his appearance was duly noticed, some thinking he was a miner clearing out of a neighbouring camp; others though he was prospecting the streets of Santiago with a view to floating another company for the *Bolsa* (Stock Exchange).

The horse was tired long before the end of the day and William had to dismount and lead him for a considerable distance, but Chilean horses are not used to being led and this one gave considerable trouble by jibbing. Later on he became almost unmanageable at times.

Colina was a filthy little hole with a rotten pub; even the horses had bad food and bad accommodation. The escort was there waiting. He had a poor horse which was tired but looked in hard condition.

I visited Colina seventy-four years later when it had become a pleasant place for a day's outing. Hot spring baths had been built including individual indoor baths and a large open-air swimming pool. There was a large refreshment/relaxation area with comfortable armchairs, but all this had been completely ruined by the mud falling down the mountains during the recent exceptionally heavy rainfall. The baths were covered in mud up to 5 feet in depth and every piece of furniture and equipment was ruined. The bonus of the rains was that the desert, further north at Serena, had come into full bloom and many Chileans went there during the 18 September Independence Day celebrations to marvel at the beautiful sight.

Friday, 10 July. The intention was to ride to Los Andes but it was too far for the horses so they stopped at Chacabuco. William stayed the night with the Administrator of the Funda who looked after him very well. He was an Austrian man who the guide said had a bad reputation. All talk that evening avoided any topics akin to war.

Saturday, 11 July. The kind host tried to get William to stay on for a few days. In the end he showed William a short cut along a private road which saved a few miles. This road petered out as they crossed the pass over the mountain, which seemed high and steeper than the surrounding peaks. The going was hard, the tracks indifferent and the country was covered in low scrub with some scattered tall cactus. The descent the other side was worse than the ascent.

They stayed in Los Andes until 16 July. During this time William made a number of expeditions into the country looking out for another suitable horse. Three short rides were undertaken to harden

the horses for the heavier work to come, and by now the guide was suffering badly from saddle sore about which he moaned considerably. The roads were very bad and after heavy rain on 14 July they became abominable.

Thursday, 16 July. William decided it was time to move on and hoped the weather would improve once they were on the road. The ride to San Felipe was utterly miserable and they were very willing to stop there for lunch. By nightfall they reached Putaendo, by which time the guide was getting badly on William's nerves for slacking.

The next section of the route was expected to contain some hard going and William thought that taking his heavy baggage would make a great difference to his comfort.

Friday, 17 July. William spent the day looking for a baggage horse and he bought a very fat gelding for seventeen pounds. It was more difficult finding a pack-saddle but he found one eventually which in due course proved to be more trouble than it was worth.

Saturday, 18 July. There was a long delay in the morning fitting the baggage. Before they had ridden half a mile, and then frequently for the rest of the day, the baggage kept slipping and had to be refitted. To add to the difficulties, instead of taking the easy route they took a short cut which involved a very severe climb instead. On arrival at the proposed destination for the night it was found that all the houses had been burnt down, including their accommodation, so they rode on for several hours in forbidding-looking country, totally devoid of habitation or cultivation. The horses were exhausted by the time they came across two little cottages which were absolute hovels, but where they could buy food for the horses and give them water. They were unsaddled and left to rest. Rather than go into the hovel William prepared to sleep outside in his flea-bag, but he was then warmly welcomed and almost forced to enter one of the hovels which, from the outside

appearance, he expected to find crawling with vermin. Despite the mud floor, the inside was spotlessly clean. He had a clean bed with clean sheets, clean table-cloth and a well-cooked dinner of six courses. It was 'one of the most welcome and best meals of my life', he wrote.

Sunday, 19 July. In the morning it was still wet but they had a good breakfast and went away with very pleasant memories.

The map again led them badly astray, many of the houses and tracks shown were either inaccurate or did not exist. They reached Chincolco that evening without mishap.

Monday, 20 July. To rest the horses a bit they hacked 10 km to Petorca and back. It was a large town about 25 km from the nearest railway to which it expected to be joined one day.

Tuesday, 21 July. Next day they were going to Llimpo but quite early William discovered his maps and torch had somehow disappeared from his saddle-bags. Having previously studied the map fairly well he decided they should move on, much to the guide's

Petorca – a halt on the Putaendo trail

annoyance as he was hating every moment of it. They reached Cuesta Bonita at lunchtime, where a local man told the guide the proposed route was unsafe so they tried his suggested route. Soon they were away from the broad well-defined track and were hunting for an almost non-existent trail buried in the snow, and after much climbing they found themselves going round in circles. The guide then said he was not sure where he was and thought he was a bit lost. It was too late to turn back and proceeding further that night could bring further difficulties, so William decided to head for the coast and low ground to the east, knowing there was a valley within easy reach where there should be a main road to Salamanca.

It was easy to find the valley but the sides were very precipitous and there was no sign of a main road. They crossed the trail they had started on in the morning but it was too late to follow it again now. As they rode through the valley the going got worse and night fell with no sign of human habitation. The guide was desperate and kept going off on imaginary tracks until he disappeared completely; it was after dark that he could just be seen on the opposite side of the gorge into which the valley had developed. Usually he was an optimist concerning houses and roads (all of which he considered as very good), but work was invariably very difficult. He considered that in the dark the going was too difficult for him to join William, so William had to try and join him. It was unpleasant scrambling and slithering down a steep and snowy slope into a fast-running stream, the bottom of which could not be seen or reconnoitred. On the other side was an equally steep scramble up.

Once rejoined they soon found a clearing in the shrubs and snow and started to bivouac for the night. While the guide lit a fire William climbed to the highest point to look for signs of human life, but there were none. On hearing the sound of musketry William quickly returned to the bivouac to find the guide defending himself against a dangerous animal that was attacking him, although on closer examination he found he had shot a skunk. The guide was by now extremely nervous and thought he would be attacked

by bandits, mountain lion or pumas. He was also very hungry, having eaten all their sandwiches after breakfast and before even starting the day's ride. He had lost or eaten their iron rations and now had William's very limited reserve supplies. William then went to bed in his flea-bag and had a good night's sleep. The guide was warm enough but too nervous to sleep, every few minutes having to look out for suspected dangers.

Wednesday, 22 July. In the morning it transpired the guide had lost most of his equipment during the last stages of the ride so he went back to find it. The shot skunk had also somehow disappeared.

Once on the trail again the guide resumed his wild dashes for imaginary tracks and by nine o'clock had completely vanished while leading William's riding horse. William meanwhile spent much time looking for the guide while leading the packhorse which was very reluctant to move on the slippery rocks. Walking up and down the steep slopes on foot in search of the guide was fruitless, dangerous and likely to result in an accident. William therefore decided to go down the valley again, still very steep and difficult, but it was now below the snowline. The baggage kept moving, and early in the day the horse slipped on some ice and sustained a very sore back from the subsequent somersault. Several times he was on the point of abandoning his baggage, but the horse would decide to go on decently for a few yards, encouraging further efforts. Eventually the valley opened out and he reached the first habitation, described as 'a filthy little hovel, inside and outside'. There the hosts fried a couple of eggs in a pan that seemed full of dirt and disease, but having had nothing to eat since breakfast anything tasted good now. After having some soup he went to the stream and drank buckets of icy cold water from the melting snows above. The horse, meanwhile, was equally enjoying his 'filthy dirty, verminous and mouldy straw'.

Just as William was about to move on again the guide suddenly appeared. He still had the riding horse and was very pleased with himself. He had travelled faster and further than William and only

dismounted once to get a meal and have a drink at a nice house he had found some distance further down, and which he thought suitable for the night. This was the time when William regretted his Spanish was totally inadequate to express his feelings.

They set off down the valley to find the fine house the guide had described and found it was another hovel, a little better that the one they had just left, so here they slept for the night, about seven in one room. The others seemed to be the most villainous cut-throats William had ever met. He kept his pistol in his hand from the moment the light went out until daylight. Sleeping out in the snow was preferable to sleeping in this company.

These 'hovels' were usually timber sheds with a corrugated-iron roof and were in various stages of disrepair. Sometimes three sheds made up a home, one each for living, sleeping and cooking.

Thursday, 23 July. It was with relief they set off in the morning and shortly after midday they reached Salamanca.

Friday, 24 July. This was to be a day to look after the horses. They were given plenty to eat and were reshod. Shoeing in Chile did not go according to the book. The frogs were cut very heavily but no-one could give a reason for this. Later, at Lonquen, William tried reshoeing a horse according to English standards with most unsatisfactory results – the horse developing a spongy and stinking frog about two weeks later. Heavy cutting then restored the hoof to its normal state quickly.

25/27 July. For the next few days William suffered from an incredible thirst and luckily the only drinks he could get were non-alcoholic.

The heavy baggage was sent by train to Illapel. The horses were now very fit, except for their sore backs, and they rode fast on the short road to Illapel. On arrival William was greeted by the local *carabineros* who were mounted and lined up in the square to meet him. He then had an armed escort to take him to the residence which had been reserved for him to stay for such time as he

honoured the town with his presence. This sudden and unsought glory was far more expensive than his ordinary simple manner of living. He then had to inspect the ranks and was warned not to check too many of the company as it was a railway one, and as such a dismounted one – all the horses had been borrowed from local people for the occasion.

The turnout was not smart, none of the horses had been groomed and the saddlery was dirty; there was a shortage of spurs, pairs being divided to make sure everyone had at least one. It was a misguided but very well-intentioned effort.

Tuesday, 28 July. They planned to leave at ten in the morning for an easy ride to a *hacienda* (hovel) nearly halfway to Combarbala, but the guide turned up two hours late. Once on the track they rode fast and covered about 20 miles in three hours. After another hour there was still no sign of the house and William realized it was another error on the lost maps. There were a few hovels, all of which appeared too dirty, and as the hill ahead did not look too steep, and Combarbala was on the other side, they moved on expecting to arrive at about eight at night.

By 8.00 p.m. they had completed four hours climbing, had just reached the snowline, and it was still another two hours before reaching the summit, so they both led their horses through the ascent which left them in good condition for the rest of the journey. In broad daylight the scenery was rather dull, but that night, in brilliant moonlight and covered in snow, it was lovely, the air was delightfully fresh and there were a few foxes to be seen.

The descent was taken at a much faster pace than would dare be attempted in daylight and they reached Combarbala at 11.45 p.m. It took fifteen minutes to get the horses under cover and fed, and they just managed to get some food at the local club before it closed at midnight – actually nearer 1.00 a.m.

Wednesday, 29 July. In the morning William saw some chinchilla

furs and he had a long haggle over them, the first he had seen outside the expensive stores in Valparaiso and Santiago.

They started at 1.00 p.m. for El Greque, a small village about 40 km away. After some difficulty obtaining accommodation a schoolmaster gave them a most effusive welcome. It was a very amusing evening. The daughters did all the waiting at table and none sat down until everyone was served, when they took their seats and entertained the guests. After dinner the table was cleared, glasses replenished and from then on the old teacher's friends came trooping in one by one. There was round upon round of drinks, while the ladies played the guitar and sang. Soon they were all singing and then they danced the national dance, the *cueca*. William danced with three specially selected daughters in turn. In the small over-crowded room with a very appreciative audience, the atmosphere was already very thick, but in such a restricted space it was impossible to maintain even a shred of dignity. No-one got to bed before midnight.

Thursday, 30 July. It was hard to get away next morning, no payment would be accepted, and they could only go when they promised to return soon.

There was hardly any track to La Paloma so they negotiated most of the 60 km by compass. La Paloma was the dirtiest village William had ever seen in South America, being even worse than Payta or Colina. The place was also infested by a most blackguardly-looking gang of ruffians.

Friday, 31 July. They were surprised and pleased to get away next morning without even losing a horse.

Sunday, 2 August. After a long ride they reached Ovalle that evening where they discovered it was Sunday. On entering the town William met an Englishman and was able to speak in English for the first time since leaving Los Andes.

Monday, 3 August. Next morning the guide reported his horse as unfit to travel any further. On inspection William found a nasty swelling on one fetlock, so the departure was postponed for several days and as time went on he became increasingly certain that the guide was deliberately maiming his horse, having already changed it once with a *carabinero* company. His ideas of horsemanship were shocking, he never tried to save his horse under any conditions and his treatment of the present injury was clearly inflaming it.

William had had enough and paid the guide well, including the fare to return his horse by train. Within half and hour of William's departure the guide left in the opposite direction at a smart canter on the horse that could only put three legs to the ground!

William anticipated no dangers on the road for some time to come as the local *banditti* had just been shot up badly. But the chief of the local *carabineros* thought otherwise and as William was under their protection he made wonderful arrangements for William to be relayed along the road. The first man did not turn up in time, so after waiting half and hour William moved on alone. The escort caught up a long time later and said he should have waited an hour for him to arrive. His relief, and others later, all met on time but at inconvenient places. As they worked in pairs food and tips become expensive.

After a day's ride of 116 km William reached Coquimbo. The nearest stables were a mile and a half from the hotel. A week was spent there planning the continuation of the ride to Antofagasta, but water supply throughout was difficult to obtain, and even to reach Copiapo there were three stretches of over a hundred miles without water. In the end William decided to get a boat back to Valparaiso. It was a small and uncomfortable boat sold by PSNC as being insufficiently seaworthy for trips to Europe. The horses resented the slings for embarking and disembarking and bore the marks of rough handling for some time afterwards.

The shipping company tried to charge very heavily for handling the horses, causing much delay in getting them ashore, so William

Coquimbo Bay

told the agent he would write to the company about it later. This satisfied the agent and William rode off. Later the company raised no objection when he declined to pay their charges.

William could not get out of Valparaiso quick enough. The horses were a bit stiff despite the sea being quite smooth, but he rode the 45 km before reaching Casablanca at a reasonably early hour.

Sunday, 9 August. It was another rainy day for the ride to Melapilla. To avoid showers William either pushed ahead or held back, and the ride became very tiring.

Monday, 10 August. The last lap of the ride was to Lonquen and it was still raining. The Maipu river was in flood. The big horse managed to cross the river easily with William on his back, but the smaller horse with the baggage was swept off his feet, and William had to hold on to the leading reins very tight to save him from being carried away. The worst part was only a few yards wide but the water was over six feet deep and swirling a lot. Although his breeches and saddle-bags were full of water, they dried quickly when the sun came out between showers.

After crossing the river William met a very drunk Chilean who was endeavouring to remount his horse. William did not assist him as he wanted to cross the river, and was very likely to drown in the process.

William had returned from a 900-mile ride during which he had kept well and the horses were very fit and hard. They drew many remarks from local people who could not believe they had covered such a distance. Chilean horses are very tough and survive conditions that many other horses could not endure.

Tuesday, 11 August. William went to see the Minister in Santiago again and learnt that the Ford affair had been settled with the Bolivian Government as far as he was concerned. This was a good ending to a fantastic ride during which he learnt much about the country and its inhabitants.

The End of Ford

It was not until September 1925 at the Legation in La Paz that William heard more about Ford's activities. He had opened his career of crime in Belgium where he had stolen an aeroplane loaded with cocaine. While Ford was loading his cargo a gendarme foolishly got in the way and was instantly shot dead, so he had to leave in a hurry. Ford landed on the Downs in Sussex, collected his cargo and left the plane to be returned to the owner by whoever it might be, at the discretion of the police. He got away with several other stunts before going on his first visit to Bolivia where he came under suspicion as being a man liable to indulge in any form of smuggling. It was left to the Bolivian representative in London to oppose his return to the country, which he did by peaceful methods at first. Once he had landed in Chile they took more active measures, but neither the Chilean nor the Peruvian government were inclined to add to the troubles of William's party.

Now William began to see the truth about the cable stating that Ford was a dangerous man.

After Ford and Peacock had flitted across the Chilean/Peruvian border, Ford spent the next few months in and out of prisons, the usual offence being obtaining money by false pretences. He eventually ended up in Arica completely broke, where he and Peacock cashed dud cheques for the return journey home, trying to travel first class, but their credit was not good enough. They suffered some hardship in Peru and indulged in a number of criminal actions. Ford was credited with palling up with a man who fell ill while on a mountain trail where he fell unconscious – Ford stole his money and deserted him. The man recovered and when he was later in Arequipa he heard that Ford was in prison. The man still thought the best of Ford and assisted him to get out of prison, whereupon Ford touched him for another hundred pounds.

The story about Ford is concluded in the following letters.

30 April 1923. The British Legation, Santiago sent a letter to William saying:

> The Acting British Chargé d'Affaires simply repeats that the President of the Republic refused absolutely to reconsider the decision arrived at, on the strength of a telegram from the Bolivian Consul General in London. I may mention that your case was not unknown to me before your visit to this Legation, but on looking up my files I find that mention is made of a Mrs North who presumably is travelling with your party.

He thought the Bolivian Consul had acted wrongly but as William had the correct visas he should be able to get straightened out.

The others would have a bigger problem.

4 May 1923. Ford wrote to William as follows:

> I have received no communication from you since you left Arica for Valparaiso. Hodgins has left the partnership and withdrawn his

money like yourself. Peacock has also left the partnership. Hodgins has refused to advance any of the £20 which you asked him to pay towards the horses we have brought here. Under these circumstances the partnership is invalid and I am instructing my solicitor in London to refund you any monies due.

14 June 1923. The Foreign Office in London wrote to Major Chads requesting a visit from him regarding the Bolivian authorities' refusal to grant his son entry as he had some fresh information. He saw him next day and was told that Ford was refused a permit for suspicion of trading in cocaine but no charges were made. Also he and Mrs North had not complied with Bolivian Consular regulations. If William worked independently the British Government would press his case for entry.

26 July 1923. The Foreign Office wrote again to Major Chads at 91 Ashley Gardens, SW1, as follows:

I am directed by the Marquess Curzon of Kedleston to inform you that His Lordship has now received a note from the Bolivian Minister in London stating that his government have decided to permit Captain Chads to enter the country. Signed. George Mounsey.

9 September 1923. William's mother wrote saying:

Four days after the Lobos sailed the Bolivian Consul got a wire stating a party with passports not in order was on board, en route for Bolivia, to farm Chinchilla. The Consul wired to his Government and found no duty had ever been paid for Chinchillas coming out of the country, therefore they had been smuggled. Order was therefore at once given to stop the entry of the party to the country ... The Bolivians then made Ford a marked man ... The Foreign Office made their enquiries and found the Police had Ford under their eye for Cocaine trafficking. The Consul General said that Ford was now wanted both by Bolivia and the English Police.

10 September 1923. The Bolivian Consul General wrote to Major Chads saying that his son was detained by the Bolivian authorities owing to the fact that he was one of Mr Ford's party, and not because he, personally, was an undesirable character. The passport was duly stamped on 3 March.

14 July 1924. Letter from the British Consulate in Callao, Peru to William c/o the Bank in Santiago:

I have to inform you that I have seen Ford only once when he called at this Consulate to make a request which I was obliged to refuse. Previously the official intervention of this Consulate was requested by a man who had lent Ford money for a partnership transaction and subsequently alleged that Ford had defrauded him and left him stranded. The British Vice Consul in Arequipa wrote early last year saying that he was personally acquainted with the facts and supported the allegation of fraud. In July last year Ford appears to have got himself into trouble again in Southern Peru and I was informed officially that he was in prison in Puno accused of fraud. I do not know the result of the latter action but it is known that he had left prison before the end of that month and subsequently passed through this port on his way to England.

From private information received I learned that when Ford first came to Peru in 1922, he brought with him a letter of introduction from somebody in England from which it appeared that Ford had expiated a crime in connection with the theft of an aeroplane.

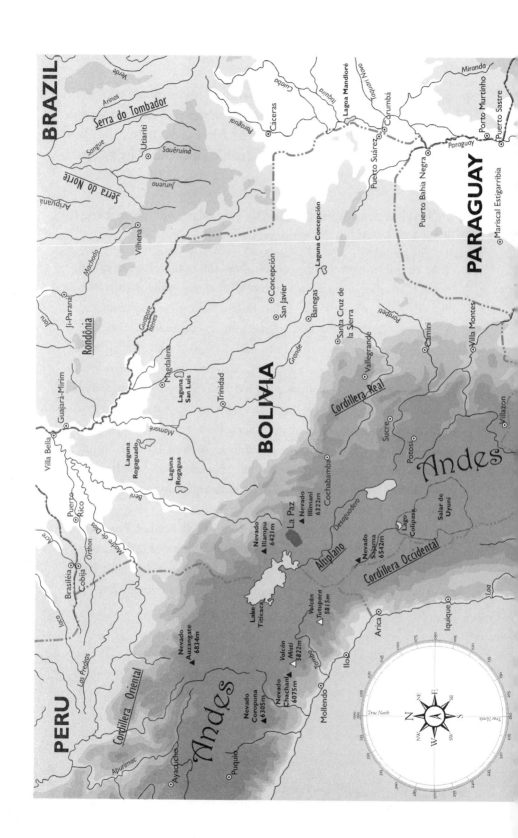

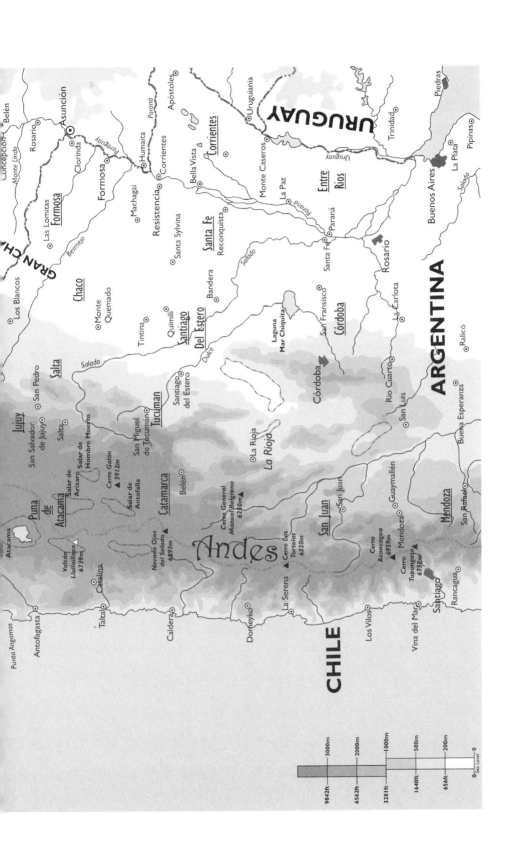

CHAPTER III

From Santiago to Asunçion and the Marsh Country

Percy the Toad

W illiam stayed at Lonquen until late September 1923, making a trip to Braden and other places of interest.

A child in the house prevented life from growing too dull. She partly earned her keep working, and one job was to clean all the women's bedrooms. In so doing she had gained much information as to the state of their underclothes. She had the knack of luring conversation into unconventional channels and often caused considerable embarrassment to unsuspecting individuals by disclosing their private skeletons to all the guests present. Egged on by Inez Foxley, a Chilean-born Englishwoman who should have known better, she started putting beetles and crickets daily into William's bath. To stop the practise William dealt with the younger one first. A fake call drew her out of the room at breakfast when no others had appeared. Her porridge was half finished, and on her return she discovered several of her insects struggling out of the remains. Feeling convinced that she had eaten a number of them, she endeavoured to be sick, and only then did William disillusion her. An armistice was easily arranged for the future. William then went on to unfold his plan for the rout of the other lady, and the fickle child without a qualm deserted her cause to assist him. William made a special journey to Santiago

where, in a restaurant, he bought the largest toad possible, a beauty, and the largest he had ever seen. In the customary manner he carried the toad off in a paper bag.

He called in at the bank on business, and there the toad made his first escape. The Manager took that particular moment to walk on the scene before he had been recaptured, and William gathered that he disapproved. On being recaptured, the bag was enclosed in a daily newspaper, in the hopes that this would be sufficiently waterproof. Ebury, an acquaintance, escorted William to the station where during a delay at the booking office, he took charge of the parcel. Further indiscretions on the part of the toad reduced the paper to pulp, and he came out for another airing. Before being recaptured William had gained a number of places in the queue awaiting tickets. The toad was offered to the booking clerk in payment for his ticket – a joke of such fine humour that he had to cease issuing tickets to go off to relate the affair to various friends, whereby William, having hastily bought two more news-papers in case of need, nearly missed the train, and some of the others were certainly late.

En route there were incidents, but no novelties. Fortunately at Lonquen William was met at the station by the child who welcomed the toad with extravagant delight, promptly christening him Percy. In an atmosphere of intense secrecy, Percy was smuggled into the house, there to be handed over to the cook to be kept in hiding until the following morning. The cook's wish to cook Percy was almost a cause of tears.

It was quite usual for this dear child to be helpful in the mornings, pouring out baths for her elders, and on the eventful morning she was at her best. At the correct hour she reported to Inez that her bath was ready, and the good lady proceeded to her ablutions well and discreetly muffled from the public gaze. Her exit a few moments later was less in accordance with propriety, opinion varying as to whether she did herself more or less than full justice. Her screams were startling, but less so than her negligée. Percy had been settled in state in a cold bath where specially selected

green stuffs surrounded him, and a liberal diet of fleas hopped on the leaves and moss for moments of hunger. It took half an hour to make the bath reasonably hygienic again. William was under suspicion as being the sole offender in this, and Inez was not on terms of any intimacy for a long time afterwards. It was an even longer time before there was any further interference with William's baths in the mornings or evenings. It was also a long time before Inez went near the bathroom again, a fact to which the child drew attention with innocent questions, the culmination of which was, 'Don't you get high if you don't have a bath?'

It was not considered right that Percy should be eaten after such a useful life, and to the cooks's sorrow, he was liberated in running water.

Some forty years later William received a beautiful drawing of a large green toad on a Christmas card from Inez. I also got to know Inez Foxley who at first lived in a very poor area outside Vina del Mar and later was cared for at Commonwealth House, a British home in Santiago. This home was very caring but run on a shoestring. When a resident had a visitor to tea and cakes the home would appoint a maid to look after the resident and her guests. At about this time Inez's nephew became Minister for Trade.

Braden Copper Mine

The ride to Braden Copper Mine from Lonquen was interesting. The Dook had offered to show William the mines any time he wished and he made excellent arrangements for William's planned visit. William rode down to the company offices in Rancagua, arriving there after dusk. Although this was said to be one of the most fertile valleys in Chile, it was too rocky to be fertile.

Next morning William was sent the 70-mile journey from Rancagua to the main camp and mill at Sewell on the company's

own railway. It was very mountainous country and the last part was almost vertical, this being climbed by a rack railway, the train being continually reversed on to lines running practically over each other. Sewell was 8,000 feet above sea level and William was to stay there for the next few days.

The bottom of the mine itself was connected to Sewell by an underground railway of between two and three miles long. All the entrances to the mine were at the bottom. They stood on empty trucks until they reached a suitable place to alight and then a lift took them up 1,500 feet, followed by a short walk and then another rise of 1,000 feet. Even at this point they were still 2,000 feet below the top workings. There were over 200 miles of shafts and galleries, prepared in three distinct levels, the top two providing the current ore while the third was prepared to take over when those above had been worked out.

The miners had a dull life living underground all day and unable to take any open-air exercise as the staff house was situated on the mountain side where ice, snow and the precipitous nature of the ground prevented any exercise.

After studying the mining methods for a week William returned to Lonquen leaving his horses to be sold by an ex-cavalryman at Braden. For several months he forgot. When he finally did try to sell the big gelding it was fat with grass. The intending purchaser gave him a good gallop at the end of which he was blowing heavily, the horse being turned down on suspicion of being in foal.

Lonquen to the Chaco

Friday, 25 September 1923. William left Lonquen and headed towards the Chaco via Santiago. There he arranged with the Anglo Bank to have funds telegraphed from England to Antofagasta. Unfortunately they sent the money by the ship after the one William had left on so he had some days to waste before he could move on.

Right: *Loading cars with ore*

Below: *Open Quarrying*

William had excellent letters of introduction which made his second evening very hectic. He was glad to get permission to go to a nitrate plant and spent two days there studying their methods.

On return to Antofagasta he collected his letter of credit and checked the places where he could obtain cash.

The railway journey across the desert was extremely boring. It passed *officina* Maria (the mining office) where he had received instruction and on the way saw a few more dotted about and lost in their vast surroundings. In the afternoon the intense heat was made worse by a hot wind and frequent dust storms made it necessary to close the windows and ventilators in the carriages.

All along the side of the railway track were pipelines bringing down the water supply to Antofagasta from the snows of Bolivia and through the whole nitrate pampa. It was distressing to see the number of skeletons of mules and horses at the sides of the track.

The train arrived at Calama at 6.30 p.m. and William got a lift for the 29-mile ride to Chuquimata in one of the manager's cars. There he stayed in the official guest house which was kept for visitors who came on business or pleasure.

Most of the workings were at a height of about 11,000 feet above sea level. The mine was an enormous undertaking, worked almost entirely by open-quarrying, big terraces on the hillside being blasted away. The continual blasting day and night was reminiscent of France during the War. The broken ore was loaded into trucks by steam and electric shovels, the largest taking up to four cubic yards at a single grab. It was a busy mine, the whole place crowded with shovels and various types of drills, and gangs of men continually shifting the railway tracks. Not far away was the plant for treating the ore. There they had an impressive mechanism for lifting complete trucks filled with ore, weighing up to 87 tons gross, and tipping it into a hopper. While the ore was falling water had to be sprayed freely to keep the dust down.

From the hopper the ore was crushed and put in huge tanks. The acid was run into accumulators and under electrical treatment the copper was deposited. The first part of the work was done

wearing gas masks. Employment was easy to get, the pay was good and because of the height leave was both good and compulsory – but William had no desire to stay.

The climate was very dry, William's camera warped badly and the leather on it and his skin began to peel off freely. Any attempt to hurry left him breathless, and even those who had been there for some time had to move slowly.

Tuesday, 13 October. William left Chuquicamate at midnight, catching the 3.00 a.m. train which arrived at Uyuni that evening. During the night the train passed through the desert, varied later on by the occasional volcano which was showing slight smoke coming out of the top, and for some hours passed through mountains. Near Ascotan the train passed the borax lakes, which appeared very white and covered a distance of 15 to 20 miles, the source of almost the whole of the world's supply at this time.

The customs at the Bolivian border were very perfunctory for both passports and baggage.

Uyuni was a sandy village with two dreadful hotels, both filthy with vile food. Sanitation was little more than what nature pro-

The borax lake, Ascotan

Llamas at Uyuni

vided. William had difficulty getting a room to himself, and having got it he had to defend it. It was the best room and during the night visitors forced their way in through the locked door with a view to doubling up. A skilfully flung riding boot was sufficient hint for them to retire making profuse apologies, which William received in such an ungracious manner they were repeated again next morning.

Here, at a height of 13,500 feet, William felt more comfortable and even played a game of tennis. That started a bout of mountain sickness which lasted a couple of days. He was constipated, had a bad head, and generally felt absolutely rotten.

Saturday, 17 October. William took the train to Atocha, 145 miles away. The last part of the route became pretty, the pampa giving way to a long ravine with occasional Indian villages and flocks of llamas.

At Atocha William bargained for transport to take him to La Quiaca on the Argentine frontier. He had considered going by mule but the tracks were washed away by the rains and he would have missed connecting trains.

It took an hour and a half to load the American touring car and get going. Besides William and his baggage it also carried four men, two women and three children. William had had no lunch on the train but one of the party in the car pressed him to accept some sandwiches. He saw them just in time to politely but firmly decline the kind offer. The rest of the party ate them gladly and some were also freely drinking red wine. Before they had covered two miles they were all extremely sick, especially the hostess and the children, remaining a stinking and vomiting mass until they reached Tupiza, the halfway halt, where they stayed for the night.

The car had to struggle through deep sand for the next 32 miles, the engine became red hot and as there was insufficient water to fill the radiator they had to wait for the engine to cool. Later in the day water was more plentiful and they crossed, recrossed and even drove along a stream. At first the splashing of water was enjoyed but the stink from the sick was still around and these splashes renewed the problem. For much of the time the road followed the railway line that was under construction to link Bolivia with Argentina.

They reached Tupiza at dusk and here the rocks were of a most striking formation, giving the impression of a mass of minarets. In view of the condition of the other passengers it was decided to stay there until Monday morning.

Tupiza was a delightful town. It was primitive in construction, all the houses being made of mud bricks and all buildings, including the church and a couple of other large buildings, had corrugated-iron roofs which shone brightly in the sun and must have been very hot to live in. The height being reduced to 11,000 feet, William was able to pass the whole of Sunday scrambling about on the rocks with his camera, firmly convinced he had found numerous silver mines.

Monday, 19 October. The party drove to Simpacha for the midday stop. The scenery was attractive in the valley, frequently winding round corners to unexpected new sights.

Tupiza valley showing Colquechaca

At Simpacha the chauffeur took the party to a hotel belonging to a friend of his where they had a dreadful meal served at a very fierce price. The Bolivians were all caught and one of them made a speech when he saw what they had to pay. Even to William's uncomprehending ear it sounded magnificent.

After lunch there were several breakdowns and luck alone enabled the party to reach the border. This time the customs were very thorough. The Bolivians at Villazon searched William and his kit, the chauffeur and the car but left the other passengers. He then had to fill in a form, and as he stated he was travelling from Chile to Chile there was much consternation and disbelief. On cross-examination William maintained he was proceeding from Santiago to Santiago and they maintained he was travelling from Bolivia to the Argentine. When they reached a satisfactory solution he was given a document to say he and his belongings were fit to leave Bolivia.

Fifty yards on they came to the Argentine customs at La Quiaca

North of Tupiza

where a similar procedure was followed but form filling came sooner. Again he was given a document of approval and went on to the hotel where more forms had to be completed. His only hope of revenge was that the authorities might try to read what he had written and learn not to molest him in future. The hotel was clean and good but they did not have a bath there.

Next morning William took the train down south and descended to a height of 7,000 feet during which he suffered earache until his ears popped – a normal occurrence in such situations. The first views of Argentina were disappointing – there were very few cattle but many slaughter houses, and crops were scarce. In the evening the train stopped at Jujuy for an hour which gave William time to look round the town, the most up-to-date he had seen for some time, with even a Ford agency.

That night was spent at Guemes, the junction for Salta. The best hotel was dreadful and the village the most filthy yet seen. The hotel tried to make William double up with another man but

he disagreed strongly and finally got a three-bedded room to himself. When William found the bedding was filthy and infested with fleas he asked for clean bedding which was considered unreasonable but was acceded to and he had a good night's sleep. The food was awful and the butter was rancid; the meat was also bad and the fish and vegetables the hotel owners pronounced unfit for human consumption.

Friday, 23 October. William left Guemes on the first possible train for Salta where he went to the bank for cash as he only had a few shillings left. The Anglo Bank had no agents in Salta, their branch in Antofagasta mixing up Salto (a small town not often shown on maps) and Salta which they thought was one and the same place. Most of the English people there were also broke, many of whom had completed contracts on the railway construction to the Chilean border but who had not been paid.

The railway had brought some prosperity to the town and they had some sugar and cattle. William was offered chinchilla furs at £80 per dozen and was told that although export was strictly prohibited it was also winked at.

At one of the houses that visitors went to for the evening for a drink and dance, they attempted to overcharge the foreigners. The foreigners rose in wrath and turned everyone out of the building, regardless of the suitability of their dress for the streets. They barricaded themselves in and the local police were sent for, deeply hurt that such a thing could happen. William slipped out of the back door and watched their efforts to force an entry, expecting a determined resistance at any moment. There was no further attempt to overcharge the tourists.

Desperate for money William took his gun to the pawn shop but the offer was so bad he never went to such a place again in South America. The hotel allowed him credit until the Anglo Bank sent him some money following some acrimonious correspondence.

William travelled to Tucuman in a Pullman car for an extra half-a-crown (2s 6d or 12½ new pence). This was an observation

Salta

carriage at the end of the train. At Tucuman this carriage was exchanged for a sleeping car which was very hot and badly ventilated. The journey to Rosario covered a vast area where wheat and flax (linseed) were grown, and some maize and alfalfa. Locusts were everywhere, many in the train, and in harvest time they would be worse.

Continuous spitting and many worse habits were common among the passengers. During the day the heat got so bad the men put their pyjama tops on because it was against the law to sit in shirtsleeves. Many seemed to make the same top do for day and night continuously for months on end.

Rosario was a modern town with a big English colony. After a couple of days, and settling his affairs with the bank, William got a flat-bottomed paddle-steamer to go upriver from Parana to Ascunçion. The river was very swollen from the rains in the north and most of the islands in mid-stream were submerged for the whole distance. The left bank of the river was from 10 to 20 feet above water level, whereas the right or west bank was flooded.

Towns and villages were far apart while the country was generally flat and open. It was very seldom that a pier of any sort was available for landing passengers or stores, the ship going alongside the bank where it was safe to do so. Usually a small boat had to be rowed out to collect passengers. In one village the entire fleet of small boats was lost from the banks crumbling and swamping the boats.

William stopped a couple of nights at Goya, a small sleepy town about halfway to Asunçion (and before the junction of the Paraguay and Parana rivers) and lying about 6 miles up a tributary of the Parana river. It was dominated by a huge statue of Liberty, presumably from the battle of independence against Spain. There were many small and very pretty birds up this tributary.

Above the junction of the Parana and Paraguay rivers the boundary between Argentina and Paraguay seemed very indefinite and they appeared to call at towns belonging to each country alternately, each town being well bedecked with its national bunting.

Near Asunçion they passed the 'Paraguayan Navy at anchor'. Formerly it was said to be capable of moving under its own steam, but now there was doubt if public money could pay for it to be towed back to its more permanent station if the moorings broke. The complete fleet consisted of two (very obsolete) river gunboats.

During one of the meals en route a man (later found to be a Frenchman) started talking about the War and made a number of disparaging remarks about the BEF. William took exception to this and through an interpreter (so that those present could understand) he made a couple of remarks. The man's dignity was offended and very soon there was trouble. He and his friends told William what they were going to do to him. After they had blown their trumpets sufficiently William suggested they would be well advised to cable England to find out his qualifications with a sword. With that the man had the impression that he had challenged a swordsman of international fame. There was only one thing he could do, he said William had completely misunderstood what he had been saying, that he had the highest opinion of the BEF

(British Expeditionary Force) and he was sorry if what he had said had been misunderstood to mean anything even slightly to the contrary.

---

6 November. William reached Asunçion where the customs had a reputation for charging everyone very highly. In the hope that the midday sun would reduce their energy, William waited to be examined last. They were, however, still full of zeal and determined to make him pay as much as possible. All foreigners were regarded as rich and therefore to be charged as much as possible. The gun and ammunition were immediately marked down for heavy duty and a slow and thorough search continued. They got completely out of hand and as a last resort he decided to rag them. He assisted them to open up his camp kit and while they searched this he set up the camp bed. In a few minutes he was ensconced in his flea-bag with a makeshift nightcap on his head and imaginary drinks beside him.

An admiring crowd of urchins had been watching the officials at work, but now they found they had something better to do. Their remarks were not accepted by the customs officers with good grace, and to add to their irritation William got out his gun and was going through the motions of shooting and cooking from his camp bed, explaining everything to them with the assistance of a dictionary, and making them find their answers the same way. He then tried to get them all in turn to assemble the gun and take it to pieces again – by this time all other searches had ceased and everyone gathered round William.

It was not long before they were most anxious to get rid of him and the jeering crowd of urchins that had collected to watch the antics of the mad gringo, who made repeated jokes at the expense of all, and were of the greatest assistance to William. He finally left in no great hurry having escaped all payment, a thing almost without precedent for a stranger with such baggage as he carried.

Some sixty or more years later, when flying to Chile while I was in transit here, I had a similar problem when they wanted to charge

customs and storage of my baggage. Throughout my transit period I was being mobbed to pay for a taxi, shoe cleaning or anything else, while the airline officials looked on with broad smiles on their faces.

William went to the Hotel Paris in Asunçion which was usually patronized by men from the Chaco. The hotel was reasonably clean and the food good, except for the soup which William refused each day. Insect life was plentiful and mosquitoes troublesome at night unless a net was available.

Many strange happenings occurred here, the most recent being only a fortnight earlier. Half a dozen wild men came in and for some unknown offence a policeman was sent to arrest them. He was chucked out, a fate which also happened to a patrol that followed. The wanted man defied the Government to take them and the Army had to be called up to besiege the hotel which the men barricaded up. For a week they sat and drank, with an occasional interruption to fire a few rounds along the street from the window. At the end of the week they were given a pardon for their offences and a safe conduct out of town and back to their native wilds, so long as they went quickly and quietly. There being no more drink left in the hotel they left and returned to the Chaco in the manner required.

Asunçion seemed to be a town full of lawless men. There were many bullet marks in the streets from recent demonstrations and revolutions. The police force seemed to be as degenerate as the majority of the population.

William was shown round the small town by his French duelling companion who bribed the senior inspector of police 10 pence to escort them round town for the day. Under his expert supervision they saw much they would otherwise have missed. At length the inspector would go no farther. They gave him a couple of drinks of *caña** but he still would not go on and handed them over to

---

* Caña is a typical South American drink and comes from sugar cane with lemon juice added. It is pure alcohol and today it is often used to run cars instead of petrol.

another man who showed them an area of foul squalor which was unsafe to be in alone or unarmed.

William had his *caña* diluted with water and added some sugar which he found very refreshing.

Asunçion is a very straggling town situated on the east bank of the Paraguay river. In the centre there were blocks of buildings which were well constructed, while moving further out the houses diminished in size with the exception of one particularly long and affluent street. Drains did not exist because the good drains that had been laid were blocked up and American experts decreed that to touch them would let loose all the foul diseases of the world. There was already typhus and many other diseases, and improved drainage could only have helped. The sick were put in isolation in the town centre, the whole block of buildings being put in quarantine, and police were posted there to see that no-one walked near or on the pavement next to the isolated houses. Most of the roads sloped towards the river and when the rains come the accumulation of garbage is carried away.

The tramlines were well laid but most were overgrown with grass and there were no trams in sight because two years earlier there was a strike for improvement in the state of the workers but the company was already insolvent.

The market was particularly smelly, all the work being done by women. During the heat of the day only women and children were to be seen and many of them were smoking the local cigars which appeared to be very strong. They carried themselves very gracefully and often had a load of some sort on their heads. William found their features rather repulsive and noted the men only turned out when it was cool and in a leisurely manner supervised the women.

The cost of living was absurdly low providing the goods were home grown. Imported food, drink and material was expensive.

On leaving the centre of town the outskirts changed quickly to become very wild and sub-tropical with many palm trees, sugar cane and bananas.

Landing stage on Paraguay river near Asunçion

The houses were widely separated and often consisted of only a waterproof dry-grass thatch with barely sufficient sticks to support it. The walls were made of widely spaced bamboo sticks to allow plenty of ventilation. Often even this amount of privacy was dispensed with. The families lived in dreadfully overcrowded conditions and child mortality was high.

In the hotel William met an amazing man who had spent the last twenty years in the back parts of the Chaco, coming to town occasionally to sell skins and feathers. The prices he obtained seemed very low yet he was making a fortune, and even more out of cattle. The skin on the back of his neck was incredibly thick and he had an amazing capacity of spitting. He could keep up a steady flow without interrupting his conversation while at mealtimes he would frequently shovel food into his mouth with his knife, and then proceed to clean his teeth with the knife without withdrawing it. He was a most interesting man to watch and to talk to, being absolutely straight and natural.

The Chaco – Rowing in the Marshes

The ship to Villa Concepcion was much smaller than the previous one to Asunçion. The scenery was similar but the marshes to the west were much larger.

In Concepcion William bought an old wide Indian punt about fifteen feet long, with short and badly balanced oars. He wanted to look at the marsh country and hoped to survive by living on his gun so he only took sugar, salt and some expensive Enos as a substitute for vegetables. He had an ample supply of disinfectant and quinine. He also took some bread which was hard when fresh and got no harder or softer with age or exposure to the weather. At first William could not bite through it, but in time he managed to, either because his teeth became sharper or his jaws stronger, and appreciated it. With plenty of spare space on board William took two bottles of *caña* and a dozen of beer – the bottles proving very useful later for holding sugar, salt and milk when the weather became bad and ants got into the boat. He took one change of clothing, flea-bag, and a sandfly net made locally and far better than the usual mosquito net. It kept out all small insects, broke the force of the showers at night and was strong enough to stand hard wear. William found it had the added advantage of his being able to see through it but could not be seen himself.

Thursday, 12 November 1923. William intended to sail at noon and it was only then that he discovered that he needed a customs pass to cross the river. The customs had an official siesta from eleven in the morning until three in the afternoon, and they had no intention of being disturbed. After great efforts he managed to get a pass and set off at one o'clock.

No maps existed of the country William proposed exploring but it was said there was a good point of entry to the marshes at Siete Puntos Riacho (seven point river) and lake, about 6 miles down-

river. As the punt drifted down the middle of the river William made the boat as comfortable as possible by storing away the baggage and food and fixing the uprights for the mosquito net at night. By sunset he was drifting on the west bank but there was nowhere to make fast for the night. He had to row across the river before finding a suitable place to moor, and it was after dark before the mosquito net was in place. A heavy shower prevented William getting a fire going and having a hot supper so he contented himself with a cold meal and was very troubled by mosquitoes the whole night through.

Friday, 13 November. William was up and dressed long before sunrise and managed to find some dry wood to make a fire for a cooked breakfast.

Within half an hour of starting he arrived at the *riacho* and crossed it. This was twenty miles downstream, not six, but from the description given this was clearly the spot he was looking for. The next few hours were a learning experience for William. He had not anticipated the strength of the currents or the difficulty of manoeuvring the boat which got stuck on an island mid-stream – there were reeds in the way and currents that twisted the boat in every direction except the one required. He had to get fifty yards upstream to clear the island but after two hours still could not make it. He drifted down to the foot of the island and had to row back up on the other side but he finally reached the entrance to the marshes. The day's journey with all that effort was only half a mile downstream and crossing the river, about a mile wide, once. A hot sun in the late afternoon dried his kit which was saturated by the afternoon showers, and in the evening he had no trouble in shooting and cooking his supper.

Saturday, 14 November. William woke at dawn. He raised himself on one elbow to look out of the punt and as his head reached the level of the sides an alligator appeared from the other side. He was not too happy about this, especially in his nightshirts, and he

quietly slipped back into bed. The visitor, appreciating his embarrassment, courteously withdrew, making no sound and hardly leaving a ripple on the water. He had been warned about the crocodiles, of which there were many, but so long as they were left alone they were not a problem.

After a good breakfast he started at six o'clock. On entering the *riacho* William expected it to be a quiet backwater but the current was very strong and progress was slow. After two hours a couple of natives passed in a canoe. They were friendly and anxious to trade some liquor but no exchanges were made.

William now had a good routine going. He had an early breakfast and tried to have himself and the boat cleaned up and to be on the move shortly after 6.00 a.m. He then rowed until 12.30 p.m. when he took an hour off for lunch. Then a further row until 4.00 p.m. when it was time to look for a camp site and any birds needed for dinner. By sunset he had everything cleaned up and was under the net and tucked up for the night.

On this third night he found a delightful camp site, had a good dinner and was in bed by 6.00 p.m. It was a beautiful night, not too hot and no insects got through the net. He was gently lulled to sleep by a chorus of frogs and the occasional heavy splash of alligators.

Sunday, 15 November. It was a beautiful bright dawn and William set off without breakfast. By 11.30 a.m. he found a suitable spot for lunch and soon had a couple of birds cooking. It was very hot and the air was still with thunder sounding in the distance. He returned to the copse where he was having his lunch and saw clouds approaching fast, so he collected branches of trees and banked up his fire to a height of 6 feet, preparing stacks of fresh wood close at hand to keep the fire going during the approaching storm. He ate the first part of his meal, and was satisfied that the boat was safe as it was pulled up on to the bank, and its contents were all stowed away safely.

The wind came in two fierce gusts, quickly followed by a strong

tornado which uprooted a number of trees on the outskirts of the copse. The sky became black for a while, and during a slight lull in the wind the rain started. At first it was really heavy. At the mission station 40 miles away they measured two inches of rain in half an hour. William was saturated and bailed out more than four inches of water from the bottom of the boat soon after the storm started. When the wind got up the fire looked as though it would burn the whole copse, but the rain extinguished it in a few moments. It was still raining two hours later but it was cooler and being so wet William felt cold. He pushed the boat back into the water and had a good row to warm up again.

That evening luck was on William's side. Instead of a dreadful wet night he found a disused hut close to the river. The roof had gone and the walls were mostly rotted away, but three sheets of corrugated iron remained which had kept one patch of ground more or less dry. The kit bag was soaked through but there remained a sufficiently dry corner of the flea-bag to allow him a good bed for the night. There was plenty more thunder, lightning and heavy rain and William had to empty water from the boat several times, each excursion getting worse as the mosquitoes had gathered in their masses and even entered the net. The skin on his arms began to peel off from the sunburn and it was not until 3.00 a.m. that the weather improved, the moon came out and the insects cleared off. By now even the frogs were silent.

Monday, 16 November. From dawn it was obviously going to be a hot day. Not having eaten the previous night William cooked a brace of plover which were plentiful there. He hung his kit and clothes to dry.

It had been a dreadful night and now to add to his problems was the inconvenience of the absence of vegetables and the Enos proved insufficient to cope. He moved on at noon with dreadful pains in his back.

Tuesday, 17 November. Now far out in the swamps there was no

sign of land for mile after mile. The whole area was covered by waterlilies, reeds and giant grasses, broken occasionally by still lakes and intersected by swiftly running waterways. The water was very muddy and even among the reeds it was impossible to touch the bottom with an oar. Most of the roots were over twenty feet long. This tangled underwater jungle was thick and impossible to drive the boat through, the only possibility being by means of the regular channels. Many of the smaller and less swiftly running channels ended in small lakes with no other exit. It was like a maize and although there were plenty of waterfowl and duck about it was hard to approach them and if one had been shot it would be impossible to recover it in the reeds.

By 2.00 p.m. William found a farmhouse on a patch of dry land. The owner gave William a little maté and told him the latest news was that the current higher up in the marshes was too strong even for the Indian canoes and all the plumage birds were 50 miles inland.

He changed direction and took a more northerly course for the next few days. His camp was well out in the reeds again near shallow water and a clump of trees standing well above the surface but with their roots well below water. Feeling better for the maté William thoroughly enjoyed lolling under the net smoking and idly dreaming until it was time to have a light cold supper before going off to sleep. The world seemed a very good place in which to be living.

A very pleasant dream was rudely interrupted by a cry of 'Hi! Help, Help!' It sounded like a young English girl's voice and seemed to come from a short distance across the reeds, probably near the trees. William shouted back but got no reply. He dressed and waited for a further cry to assess the direction more accurately. Next time it was further away and William yelled back and fired his gun to announce he was coming. He started to force his way through the reeds, keeping direction by means of the stars. It was heavy going, for each time he pulled the oars the boat rose forward pushing the reeds before it, and each time he lifted the oars to

take a fresh stroke the boat slipped back to where it had last been. He then tried to pull himself forward by means of the reeds, but they came out from the bottom making progress even more difficult. He pressed on for several hours and in this time only gained about ten yards, the mosquitoes were getting forever worse, and there were no more cries. William now had to wait until morning if he was going to find this poor girl.

Friday, 18 November. It was not until the first signs of daybreak that William could get clear of the reeds, but no more calls from the girl were heard. Soon he found a channel that led to the trees he had spotted the previous night. There was no sign of a camp or canoe having been tied up there and William's expectations of finding a handful of Indians with an abducted female were fading. Suddenly, from just above his head, that cry came again. Satisfied this was the source of the cries heard overnight he shot the bird without hesitation and only regretted that it did not taste better. He heard that call again many times after that but never again did he set out to look for a distressed damsel.

The following night William made his camp at the foot of some trees with just enough dry ground on which to make a fire, he ate two birds for supper and cleaned and hung a third one from a branch of a tree ready for breakfast. It was near sunset and there seemed too little time to clean up the boat properly before the mosquitoes appeared. The boat was afloat and safe from an invasion from ants, so it was not necessary to throw disinfectant on the bloodstains left after cleaning the birds. After a happy day he dozed off peacefully.

Just before midnight William woke with a feeling of impending trouble, and panic came over him for no obvious reason. He quickly dressed and checked his weapons were in order. After a short while there was a gentle scratching on the bottom of the boat, so he stamped his feet heavily and the scratching stopped. Soon the scratching started again but this time no amount of stamping stopped it. William then tried jumping on the bottom, rocking

the boat and splashing the water with an oar, each having a little effect for a short time but always the scratching resumed more violently and persistently. It was obviously something pretty big and so it would be unwise to put an arm down to remove it. He could not risk having a hole made through the bottom of the boat, for apart from the immediate danger, he was at least a hundred miles from the nearest civilization and there was no chance of any traffic passing that clump of trees if he could not get away in his boat. He fired a shot into the water with no result and realized it was risky and liable to provoke a more violent attack. William collected his hanging bird and got on the move as quickly as possible. The scratching had become frenzied but ceased as soon as he got under way. He rowed from 1.30 a.m. until 6.00 a.m during which time he failed to appreciate either the bewitching moonlit scenery or the infernal insect pests. He never did find out what was under the boat but presumed that whatever it was had been attracted by the smell of blood on the side and bottom of the boat from the birds. After this he always cleaned the boat up properly and never had another attack.

Saturday, 19 November. After such a night William was too tired to enjoy his breakfast. He travelled some distance further in a northerly direction and then went back into the Paraguay river, joining it much nearer Concepcion than the point from which he had left it. This saved some rowing against the current. The river had swollen considerably and it was difficult to make any progress round bends. Each time he had to cross the river (about a mile wide) he lost ground which had to be made up by hard rowing. Sometimes he would get into an easier current. The worst day was when it took over three hours to travel half a mile.

Most nights he camped on the east bank where firewood and shelter were easier to find, and during the day made a number of excursions up the small *riachos* into the Chaco.

Once near to Concepcion he decided to look at the entrance to the Rio Negro. He rowed upstream some distance above the town

and then drifted back down again doing his packing meanwhile. Whilst travelling downstream he was rammed broadside on by another boat which was heavily laden and the collision put them into more danger than William. It was being steered by the Padre of the Chaco Mission who had plenty of room to pass on either side but somehow failed to do so. They parted without too many bad words.

When William eventually arrived back at Concepcion he heard that he had been expected back several days earlier and they thought he was probably completely lost. His remaining baggage luckily remained intact – doubtless because there was another European still staying at the hotel. It was a very hot day and William spent the rest of the evening trying to keep cool by sponging himself down in a basin of nominally cold water.

Comment

Apart from suffering the inconvenience of the lack of vegetables in his diet William felt extremely fit, and a little maté soon corrected that problem. Apart from some unripe prickly pears William had seen no fruit growing. Sunburn was not too severe but insects were a considerable nuisance unless he went to bed early and remained under the net until sunrise. On occasion William had to face the

River Indians (civilized)

dreaded mosquitoes and it only took a few moments before he was unable to see his hands on account of the numbers that had settled for a feast. Luckily malaria was not too serious in this area. During the day a large black fly produced painful stings which penetrated William's shirt, socks or whatever else it settled on, although it did not pursue him in the shady places where the mosquito lurked.

Small red ants were everywhere and quickly found the sugar and milk. By using disinfectant freely and putting the sugar and milk into stoppered bottles reduced the temptation for them to remain on board. Snakes were to be seen and looked thoroughly dangerous but they never threatened William. Throughout the trip he saw very few humans and was disappointed at the scarcity of animal and bird life. Sometimes at night there would be continuous splashing, but he only saw a few alligators, some water-hogs and a seal of sorts, although many other animals were said to exist in the area.

Along the main river, especially, there were large numbers and many varieties of parrots and kingfishers. They were all very noisy and the latter seemed very tame, often following William for as much as half a mile along the river. In the marshes there was a large kind of turkey which he concluded must be good eating because they were hard to shoot, but was later told their precautions were more due to vanity rather than taste. In daylight hours they would fly every few minutes to the highest tree or shrub in the neighbourhood to look out for possible danger, showing a great sense of safe and unsafe country. William only once got near enough to attempt a shot, and missed.

He also had the company of a beautiful waterfowl which followed him for a mile or so shrieking and disturbing all other game in the area, which was not good for the pot and saved many other more tasty birds from that fate. Ducks were scarce and tended to be in places where had they been shot they could not have been recovered. The need for food rested with the poor plover. They seemed to have a hopeless yearning to be shot, and at the sight of

a gun they flew round in small circles bleating and almost trying to dash out their brains on the muzzle, at the same time scaring off the other birds. There were few small birds.

The only other source of food was fish – apparently it was possible to catch fish up to a couple of hundred pounds in weight but William only succeeded in catching a few minnows in a handkerchief. Several times he managed to lose hooks and he lost his bait on many occasions.

When he got near Concepcion he saw native fishermen at work and noted their tackle was composed of a stout pole to which was attached rope an inch in diameter, a chain or something stouter. Hooks and bait were in proportion, and with this formidable weapon they drifted downstream literally flogging the river. Some of the fish caught in this manner were very big and were at once suspended by a rope round their tails with their heads hanging in the water; in this position they were kept alive for a long time and reached the market fresh.

In some parts the water was infested with piranha which made bathing dangerous. This small voracious fish abounds in South American fresh waters and is extremely dangerous. Cases were told of men falling from a river steamer and having their bones picked bare before help could reach them. William did once risk a plunge into the river but clambered out again as fast as possible. He did his ablutions in a canvas bucket for greater safety.

At sunrise on one particular morning he was washing with the boat well hidden among the reeds, out of sight of the nearest waterway. Shaving was well in progress and he had a fine lather on his face, which was, incidentally, the only covering he had at the time. He heard a faint sound near him and stood up in the boat to see what it was. To his surprise he saw two Indians coming towards him in a canoe and they were by now quite close. As soon as they saw William standing there they cleared off at top speed. He then sat down laughing at their probable thoughts on seeing him in that condition. It was not long before they returned with

many others and they seemed surprised not to find a river god there who could stand on water.

All the natives William came across were interested in him as a white man was a rarity. His attempts to take photographs were regarded with the gravest suspicions and had to be treated with due care. Similar suspicions also occurred in Africa where cameras where not familiar.

The scenery throughout the trip was very wild and most of the camping sites were in perfectly delightful surroundings. The heat was terrific – so much so that William could heat water in a bottle at midday by reflecting the sun's rays on to it by means of a mirror. In this way the water became too hot to touch with the bare hand.

CHAPTER IV

The Ride to the Chaco

On the Sunday after returning to Concepcion William accompanied the Mission padre across the river to see some of his natives of the Lengua tribe who were encamped opposite the town on the Chaco side of the river.

The quickest way across the river was considered to be via the island, crossing two stretches of water. The island was about a mile and a half wide, and at one point there was a formidable barrier of mud, which was said to be passable by means of planks. On this occasion William and the padre had to be carried across it on the back of an Indian who kept his feet in a wonderful manner in the slime.

The design of the Mission caravan proved to be of a most serviceable type. The carts were very solidly built, with wheels 6 feet in diameter, to give them a chance of getting past the various obstacles they were liable to meet on their journeys. The hoods were made of anything – corrugated iron, hides, branches of palms or whatever came to the carpenter's hands. The singing by the natives in the church services was quite good.

Before returning to Villa Conceptcion William made arrangements with Kennedy, the manager of an *estancia* (farm ranch usually with a vast area of land), to sleep at Rio Negro for that night and to ride out with him into the Chaco the following morning. Because no baggage horses were available and as most of the route was a foot or so under water, William was asked to travel as light as possible. He therefore confined himself to a pair of light saddle-bags – a mosquito net was the only item Kennedy considered essential – a single change of underclothing, toilet essentials, a small camera,

a gun with a few rounds of ammunition and a very light numnah saddle (made of something similar to felt underlay rather than a large leather saddle).

With these bare necessities William started back across the river shortly before dusk. On the island he reached the muddy patch easily. Rather than try to ford it, he tried to find a simpler way round. The island was several miles long and intersected with many deep dikes. These were impossible to cross while carrying the baggage, and were too wide to be able to throw the kit across and then jump. Darkness came on very suddenly. To make matters worse there was a heavy thunderstorm with vivid lightning constantly flashing all around. William covered many miles before deciding it was time to retrace his steps and return to the muddy crossing where he soon found a guide to take him the rest of the way. As soon as the storm stopped the mosquitoes came out and on this occasion he longed for another storm to get rid of them. He reached Rio Negro camp about 9.30 p.m. at night, ready for supper and a good night's rest.

The trek to the Chaco was to start at dawn. The night was very hot, the bed singularly uncomfortable, so it was not difficult to be ready for the proposed early start at 5.00 a.m., but owing to difficulties in rounding up the horses they were not on the road until 7.00 a.m. The party consisted of William, Kennedy and five Indians who were driving about forty unbroken horses ahead of them.

For the first twenty minutes they trotted steadily through long grass. The horses in front put up myriads of mosquitoes, horse flies and midges – a trial which lasted throughout the day. At this point they reached the first marsh, through which they had to walk, and where they saw the first cattle for which the district is known. From here on they saw many thousands of cattle.

At 9.00 a.m. they passed a native fishing village near the banks of the Rio Negro which they had to cross for the first time. The horses were driven into and across the water by throwing clods of earth at them, and it was not easy to round them up again on the

other side. The men and saddlery were taken across in a small punt. Two miles on they came to Loma Ponar, an *estancia* where they stayed for an hour to rest and have a drink.

They left at 10.30 a.m. and after another hour's trot arrived at the bigger marshes and saw the first of the egrets, which were as large as small storks and far bigger than any William had seen in London Zoo. They were very shy and looked rather ungainly standing out in the long rank grass. From now on there was a great variety of bird life, mostly large birds, some with particularly beautiful colouring. Cattle were increasing in numbers and most were not branded. Many of them were only handled to be branded once in five years during which time they became completely wild. The water was generally over a foot deep so Kennedy tried to keep to high ground by trotting round the marsh areas where possible.

By 1.00 p.m. they reached a small well-fenced shack where they had their halfway halt with lunch and a good rest. It was normally maintained for resting cattle that were being driven into the Mataderos from the interior. The Mission caravan was also parked there, with goods to the value of well over a thousand pounds being entirely under local black supervision.

The heat was terrific, and a slight breeze seemed to make it hotter than if there had been no wind at all but reluctantly at 4.15 p.m., they decided to move on, all the Indians having changed their horses.

The second and rather longer half of the day's run was a little faster than during the first part. By sunset the scenery looked attractive with many palm trees with a brilliant sky for a background, while on one side was a wood in which the egrets were going to roost. They arrived in thousands in slow flight, looking like a number of white crosses against the blue sky as they flew over.

Travelling in the dark brought the usual problems from mosquitoes and at frequent intervals they ran into spider's webs between the trees. Some of these were so strong they cut their faces. On closer examination later William found they contained several hundred

spiders, each about the size of a penny (50 new pence piece), which accounted for them being so strong.

They reached their destination at 9.00 p.m. by which time it was very dark. It was the first long ride William had undertaken for several months and for the final hour he was sore and very tired. Riding to the houses on the *estancia* necessitated going over a footbridge in complete darkness with no handrails and a big drop on either side – an unnerving end to a long day. He was absolutely soaked with perspiration, including his breeches. His ammunition belt made it seem hotter and as he carried a gun in one hand he had no possibility of driving off the mosquitoes, who enjoyed an undisturbed feast all day.

The *estancia* consisted of a group of seven wooden houses sited in a clearing in a wood out of sight of the palms which grew very monotonous after a while. A few hundred yards away there were two native shacks into which ten native families were squashed, without even considering themselves overcrowded. Beyond the wood the marsh extended for miles in all directions, usually the ground being covered by a foot of water and with occasional fences to bound the huge paddocks enabling the men in charge to control the feeding grounds of the cattle.

Men in the Chaco

The following morning William spent three hours on foot in these marshes trying to shoot some birds, but nothing came in range except some bleating plover which he was not inclined to kill, and there were no egrets in sight. After tea he went out again, this time on horseback with Kennedy to see cattle being rounded up and moved to fresh grounds. By 5.00 p.m. the egrets started rising everywhere and flying to a wood to roost. William crawled up closer to see many of the trees bending under the weight of their numbers. When they had settled he fired a round from his gun. The birds rose in their thousands and circled round and round over the wood but none went to another roosting place. Having shot a couple of birds it was dark and time to return to the *estancia*. They rode at a fast trot but as William's hands were occupied carrying the birds the insects again attacked him relentlessly. He had to trust his horse to follow Kennedy's, mainly by sound, as Kennedy's head was below the level of the grass for most of the time. It was a dreadful ride back and the horses deserved great credit for maintaining the pace without falling.

On other nights William again tried firing a single shot into the air to see what happened. Sometimes it put up many birds, especially duck and geese, and he could have had some wonderful shooting had he had an ample supply of ammunition in good condition, but the few rounds he had deteriorated very rapidly in the severe climate.

For the return ride to Villa Concepcion William was given the services of a mounted Indian guide. They made a late start, but considering the conditions they rode very fast and made up an hour in the first half of the day. The halt was much shorter and the guide elected to ride straight ahead through the marshes, the water being well over the horses' knees, and never attempted to skirt round the edges at a faster pace. The second half of the day was much slower. After the halt the weather became threatening and early in the afternoon heavy squalls broke, a loud clap of thunder sending thousands of cattle stampeding past within a hundred yards – a very impressive sight. The storm lasted about

an hour, during which time the rain was so heavy that many birds lay on the ground unable to rise, looking so frightened and helpless they could easily have been caught by hand.

The continued driving rain was such that at times it was impossible to see more than a few yards ahead, though the wind was a good enough guide to show the required direction. The guide (who must have been upset by William's determination to proceed) and horses were in favour of turning their backs to the storm and making for the nearest shelter, but William had booked his passage on a boat and could not delay.

By 4.00 p.m. the weather cleared and the sun came out again. William was now in the midst of thousands of birds. The blue heron was particularly conspicuous and there were many storks and flamingos, the latter looking very pretty in flight in the sun. The egrets had greatly increased in numbers and had moved much closer to the river.

Back at Loma Ponar again William rested for an hour before hurrying on to cross the River Negro at dusk. The guide was very frightened of the dark and set a smart pace which even William found hard to match. They reached their destination at 8.00 p.m. William was by now in a particularly filthy condition and even the rain failed to clean up the blood on his breeches which were in a revolting state. His shirt, pants and socks were all in ribbons, his tie was torn away and the sole of one boot, which was ripped off, had been tied roughly in place again with a bit of string. William's attempts to wash his clothes in the muddy water made them look even worse than they were before – only his gun remained clean.

Comment

This trip was made over a vast grassy plain with occasional clumps of wood and belts of palms. The standing water showed how only a couple of feet difference could constitute high ground. In the first 20 or 30 miles from the Paraguay river the grass had all been grazed over and regrown to a height of about 5 feet. Further inland

the virgin country carried grasses over 12 feet high – well above the heads of mounted men. Fires had reduced the height in some places and improved the quality of the grass.

In the first 10 miles from the river there appeared to be only palm trees, other trees all being further inland. Undergrowth in all the woods made them impassable except by the tracks cut through by the Mission.

The climate was expected to be wet for half the year, during which time the ground carried much standing water. The remaining six months were complete drought. Occasionally the droughts lasted for eighteen months and this caused considerable anxiety over the water supply for cattle. Many cactus in the woods carried up to a pint of beautifully fresh cold water through the severest droughts, which could be easily tapped with a knife. The palms were only used for fuel and fencing, though the hearts of some were said to be fairly nourishing if eaten while very young.

Boundaries in South America had long been open to dispute and the boundary between Bolivia and Paraguay was no exception. William thought that since the Indians were very liable to kill nationals of either country on sight, it seemed rather an unnecessary international controversy.

The English had a great reputation to live up to in this region due largely to the excellent pioneer work of the first missionary, called Grubb, who was not a cleric. He wrote a book, *An Unknown People in an Unknown Land* describing the place some years earlier. It was very little out of date in 1923, and those who knew the country best said that it was very accurate in detail.

Up to a month previous to William's visit the English had the reputation of never dying, then at the end of the drought two youngsters got lost. One died of thirst shading his head under a big cactus which held plenty of water, although the boy had a knife in his pocket; while the other died of starvation and general weakness within a mile of his camp, but omitted to light a smoke fire to show the native rescuers who were out looking for him where he was lying.

Bovril, Fray Bentos and other similar concerns purchased a lot of cattle in that region. The average price seemed to be about one pound sterling per head for mixed cattle. Foot and mouth disease was prevalent but was almost completely ignored as it was thought to be only fatal to calves. There was another unidentified disease that attacked horses, and they had to be restocked every year or eighteen months.

The food William was presented with during this trip was unlike anything he had ever tried before. First there was *charqui*, or dried meat, made by salting long strips of fresh meat and hanging it up to bake in the sun for several days. It was then taken in and hung on rafters in huts or houses until required, with no protection from vermin or flies. Lumps were hacked off and carried in the pocket or any more hygienic way considered convenient. Even after prolonged stewing in soup it was still hard but with healthy appetites it tasted good. It kept for a long time and I remember not being very impressed when I had a bite of a piece some twenty years later.

Bread was of the same sort as William had on the boat trip. Knives had to be sharp to cut either the bread or the meat, and teeth improve wonderfully under such conditions – everyone around seemed to have excellent teeth.

The puddings served were often very sweet and usually eaten with the local cheese. Marmalade in a sandwich of *mandioca* cheese instead of bread made a nice and appetizing dish – although in different circumstances William might have looked askance at it. (*Mandioca* (cassava) is a tropical plant containing starch or flour from which bread is made.) The order in which dishes were served up at meal times seemed to depend entirely on the order in which the cook had them ready to serve.

Glasses were scarce and one glass was expected to do for all sitting down to an ordinary meal, other than in the manager's house in an *estancia*, where each person could rely on not having to share his drink with others.

Beans, maize and fish were all liable to appear in due season.

The maize suffered greatly from depredations of the parrots, and to protect them the cobs were broken and hung down to ripen, which seemed to be sufficient to keep the birds away. The fish were usually lung fish, which were easily caught in the marshes as they came up to breathe under tussocks of grass and were usually killed with a spear. During the dry season they burrowed down into the deep mud making a damp nest well below the surface of the ground, leaving a ventilation hole for breathing. These holes betrayed the burrows and the fish when dug up from the apparently solid ground were excellent eating. The Indian children were ready to gorge to bursting point. After a heavy meal in a good season, they could hardly stand, and had no hope of walking when really full, their tummies being distended to an astonishing extent.

On return from some of these long trips William suffered the consequences of not having enough vegetables to eat and his remedy for this was maté, obtained from a small shrub which was cultivated abundantly. The leaves were treated in a similar manner to tea. A gourd was made from a hollowed-out root, into which the chopped leaves were placed and boiling water added. A few people preferred cold water. The resulting beverage was sucked up through a *bombilla* (a tube or pipe with a filter at the end). The one gourd or *bomba* and *bombilla* sufficed for any number of people gathered in a group. A child was usually delegated to pass the maté round. The first person would empty the gourd and then silently handed it back to the child who refilled it with hot water and passed it on to the next person; this continued until everyone in the circle had been served once and then the first person received the *bomba* for a second time. The drink went round and round until everyone had had enough, which was denoted by handing the vessel back to the child and for the first time saying the equivalent to 'Thank you'. At first William was too polite and missed out after the first round because he said his 'Thank you' too soon. When he realized what was happening he developed a suitable scowl when handing it back to ensure that he would not be omitted from further rounds. The taste grows on one very quickly, and among those who had

been in the country for a long time the habit had become almost a vice. Some vendors allowed twigs and other bits and pieces to get mixed in with the leaf which spoiled the flavour and added to their profits. There was another rather rare leaf which many people added to their tobacco and claimed it improved even the worst tobacco quite considerably.

The Train to Horqueta

William made one other excursion from Villa Concepcion when he took the local express train to Horqueta. The railway was marked on the map and because it seemed such an unlikely place he thought it would be interesting to explore. The train was due to start at 10.00 a.m., but William was warned that it was liable to leave at any time between 9.00 a.m. and midday, and that he should not worry if he found it had gone before he arrived at the station or left after midday. A complaint was liable to cause a lightning strike by the driver, and there was no-one else who could take his place.

On the day William travelled the train was half an hour early and made wonderful progress considering the cheapness and shoddiness of everything. When it got near to Horqueta the guard saw some friends and stopped the train while he transacted his business with them. The engine driver was introduced and by the time the train reached its destination it was barely an hour later than scheduled.

Horqueta was a very uninteresting place and William was ready in plenty of time for the return train which was due to leave at 3.00 p.m. He arrived an hour and a half early while the driver was the same amount late! Despite being this late he still waited a bit longer for his wife. When they reached the place where the friends lived (from the outward journey) the wife had to be introduced to them and carried on as if there was no reason why the three-hour journey should ever be completed. Luckily for the passengers, a

heavy storm broke and their conversations were interrupted. As there was little cover for the driver on the engine he went full speed ahead and threatened to beat all its previous records. They arrived back at Concepcion at 6.30 p.m., only half an hour late.

Three days later William was back at Asunçion where he stayed a couple of nights before taking the international train to Posadas on the Parana river. The line in Paraguay was particularly bad and although the train went at a slow rate the carriages rocked in an alarming manner. The other passengers either knew no better or were accustomed to the line, for they showed no concern and accepted it as a fine up-to-date railway. Along the route there were quite a number of moderately long halts, and at each station the knowledgeable got out and purchased the speciality of the region – be it food, rope, hammocks and the like.

Most of the journey was through forest country, Villa Rica having been a big timber town in the recent past. There was said to have been an error made there when building a railway branch line. The surveyor failed to notice a number of steep hills and designed the line to run as seemed most convenient from his office. When the track was being cleared of trees the hills were discovered and work on the line ceased. William could not be sure this story was true, but from what he saw of the country it probably was.

At Encarnacion they crossed the Parana river and the international border by means of a big ferry which carried the train and all its occupants across the river. This was judged to be safer than over a bridge in such a remote area. During the crossing the customs searched all baggage, but being late at night they put little enthusiasm into it.

On reaching the other side of the river William spent the night at a small French hotel which even boasted a shower – albeit a feeble trickle of passably clean water.

CHAPTER V

Iguazu Falls

ext morning he caught the connecting boat to take him to the Iguazu (known as Iguaçu in Brazil) river. It was a very small boat with paddle wheels at the stern to facilitate navigation in the narrower reaches of the river. The heat from the engine room permeated through the whole ship, during the day the cabins became unbearably hot and there were very few electric fans to ease the situation. Most of the passengers were Germans going to a colony they had established in the Mission country.

At Posadas the river was about a mile wide, slow running and twisting, but it soon narrowed down and became straighter. Even so it required an expert on the bridge to navigate safely past the many precipitous outcrops, often with cascades and waterfalls dropping almost directly into the main river.

It was a long trip and on the evening of the fourth day they reached Puerto Aguirre, the river junction. William disembarked at 4.30 a.m., an hour before dawn. The river seemed small and sandy and there was nothing to suggest what tremendous falls were situated so nearby. After a couple of hours wait transport appeared to take William to the Cataract Hotel, a drive of 20 km through wild forest abounding in butterflies and beautiful moths.

The Iguazu river marks the boundary between Argentina and Brazil and each country maintained a pretentious hotel just within its borders to attract tourists to the falls.

The falls are absolutely magnificent and as soon as they are seen appear to be something so beautiful as to be outside this world. They are situated in wild forest country, the undulations of the

Iguazu Falls – general view Argentine side

Iguazu Falls

Iguazu Salto del Diablo

land allowing several magnificent views of them from a long distance off – the large trees giving some indication of their great size. In the centre, and at the foot of the falls, there was an island covered with huge trees, and immediately behind this was the largest fall, the Salto del Diablo. Viewed from the hotel these trees appeared to be little bigger than shrubs, with the spray from the cascade rising high above them. The din from the falls even at that distance was considerable. William reckoned the total width to be about 2 miles, the largest volume of water falling on the Brazilian side where the river bed had worn back furthest. The drop was nearly the same throughout, about 200 feet, and most parts could be easily approached up the river bed. The Salto del Diablo alone was hard to see, partly on account of the trees immediately in front of it, and mainly on account of the clouds of spray which obscured everything. He spent many hours scrambling round the rocks seeing all that was possible and absorbing this wonderful piece of nature.

Back at the hotel William noticed there were the signatures of many American tourists who claimed to have seen both the Niagara and the Victoria falls, and all proclaimed this to be far bigger and more imposing in every way, and with the exception of the two hotels there were no buildings or public works to spoil the wildness of the view. I visited these falls on the Brazilian side in 1979, fifty-four years later, and apart from a small aircraft landing strip, the place was still totally undeveloped. My first sight of these magnificent falls brought tears of delight. I also explored the surrounding country of wild forest with not a person to be seen. After a time I felt I was walking in country where I did not know what dangers might exist and thought it safer to return.

The Leech

Thursday, 10 December 1923. William travelled with very little luggage as he continued his journey up the Iguazu river in very

hot weather. He noted the tracks ran close to the river, the water was beautifully clear and sweet, and appeared to contain no dangers – he saw no alligators or big fish, and there was a great scarcity of birds.

To counter the effects of the intense heat William carried a face towel in his hand (which he found preferable to a canvas bucket) which he used either to sponge down or to trickle water into his mouth for a gargle. He was physically very fit and did not carry a scrap of fat.

Before he had gone very far he became aware of a pain in his throat, near the larynx, which rapidly grew worse. About the same time his temperature went up suddenly, and his thoughts went back to all the foul diseases rampant in Asunçion which he had passed through a few days previously. He returned to the Cataract Hotel as fast as he could, getting in that night, by which time he had a bad headache and there seemed to be a swelling in his throat. Very slowly and with great pain he managed to swallow a little water. By the following morning, Friday, 11 December 1923 the blockage had become complete and in addition he had completely lost his voice.

By that evening his temperature was down to normal again, and he decided that it must have been due to a touch of the sun. All aches and pains had gone except the swelling in the throat, and it seemed highly probable that some bug of moderate size had gone down his throat with the water and taken lodging there.

He could not think how to shift it. Many and various were the tales that he could remember being told of the ways in which insects had entered humans and made themselves unpleasant, but this seemed to be different to them all. On thinking it all through he decided to make for the nearest reliable doctor, probably at Buenos Aires or Montevideo – in either case an awfully long journey in the circumstances.

Fortunately a boat was due to sail for Posadas next day so he arranged for the hotel cart to take him to Puerto Aguirre in plenty of time. The jolting on the rough wood track was too great and

by the time he arrived at the port he was delirious. The pain in his throat was not so bad but the irritation caused much saliva and when this got to the back of his mouth he suffered greatly. A local doctor travelling on the same ship thought he had a terrible disease, and he was nearly turned off the ship. When William saw his changed appearance in the last two days he thought there was some justification for this view.

He kept cool by sitting in the spray thrown into the bathroom by the paddles at the stern of the ship, and was far cooler than he had been during the outward journey. This had the additional advantage of reducing the need to drink and probably saved his life as by this time he could neither eat nor drink. He spent the rest of the time in bed as there was no need to attend meals.

Sunday, 13 December. On the fourth day William was spitting much blood, and it appeared that his internal visitor was either completely gorged or else he was doing considerable damage, so he decided to try a drastic remedy. Bad red wine, ice, soda water and salt were blended to obtain as cold a mixture as possible, while at the same time he fomented his throat so strongly on the outside that he burned much skin off. When everything was ready he took a big gulp of the filthy mixture which he could not swallow but things happened. It was a most revolting few minutes when he vomited up masses of blood and muck, but he knew that the bug had burst.

Monday, 14 December. Next morning he managed to drink a few drops of water without too much pain. Later in the day the ship reached Posadas where he alighted to await the train south. The ship's officers were delighted to see the last of him, being sure they were in danger of catching some serious disease. That afternoon William managed to swallow a couple of raw eggs which he found most strengthening and was able to make the necessary arrangements to catch the train south that night.

In the train he stayed in bed throughout the journey, still only able to take liquid refreshment. He shared the compartment with

a young man from Denmark who was most helpful, especially when he found William could write his language more easily than he could Spanish.

There was a continual filthy taste in his mouth and it seemed an unending task cleaning out the fur which seemed to be forming on his tongue every few minutes. There was still frequent pain, and he became delirious again. His cash had disappeared but he was in no fit state to look after it or to care what happened to it.

On arrival at Buenos Aires he felt much stronger than when he first got on the train and went straight to the bank, but his voice had not recovered and the clerk could not hear him across the counter. William tried to raise his voice, which was painful, but by so doing he just managed to make himself heard. The clerk thought his mail and cash had been sent to Montevideo. Fortunately this clerk had dealt with some of the previous correspondence and could therefore identify William. He lent William sufficient cash to get him to Montevideo to collect his mail. There was a nightly service of boats so he decided to cross that night, although there was very little time to get a visa for Uruguay and as he thought his condition was now mainly due to lack of food he postponed seeing the doctor until he got to Montevideo. In the last ten days he had lost over two stone in weight, his skin was festooned on him and his clothes were even more loosely fitting. Before the train was due to leave he attempted to eat a lightly cooked omelette but even this proved too much.

All William's baggage had disappeared but he was in no condition to see what had happened to it and thought it would probably turn up on his return. He made one further effort to find his luggage at the station but the official there would not open the baggage office to have another look and he had insufficient energy to coax the men to open it. A few soft words and a little bribery would have produced it all that night, instead of which it remained there until his return, by which time it was said to be lost.

William left Buenos Aires that night with simply the clothes he was wearing and his camera.

Sunday, 20 December 1923. The following morning William managed to eat his first bit of solid food, although it took half an hour to eat a roll of bread soaked in coffee. It was laborious as his jaw muscles seemed ineffective.

On arrival at Montevideo he went to the bank where there was mail, but no cash, and went on to the hospital, but could not see a doctor. Neither the British Minister nor the Consul would have anything to do with him, his story being too improbable to be believed.

Returning to the hospital, and after some wait, a doctor arrived who had already heard the story and regarded it most sceptically. He started his examination with a heavy hand until he saw the marks of the intruder, when his manner changed completely. He identified it immediately as a leech by the triangular shape of the bites. As it had gone by now there was nothing he could do, saying all that was needed was feeding up again. He suggested William should go to the Services Association and tell them what had happened and ask them to ring him (the doctor) to confirm the story. They listened to the story, verified it, checked his identification and then gave all the assistance they could offer. They sent off wires, booked him into a decent and clean hotel and lent him some pin money.

By now William had been ten days without solid food, and for the first five days he could not even drink water. To fend for himself he had had to trek on foot for most of one day, he had a severe shaking in the wagon from the hotel, and he was almost physically removed from the ship before reaching Posadas – and the ordeal was still not over.

Thursday, 24 December. William received a wire from Ebury, in Santiago, to say cash had arrived there but he did not receive it until 27 December, and he did not get replies to his telegrams to the bank until then either.

Sunday, 27 December. William settled up with his hotel and after

further delays got his visa renewed for Argentina, that evening taking the ship for Buenos Aires where he hoped to find his baggage. He bought a change of underwear and had tried washing his clothes in his room to save time and money while funds were so short, but they did not dry and in the morning he had to remain in bed.

William's impressions of Montevideo were rather hazy and, in his circumstances, rather prejudiced. He was surprised to find that few shops took any notice of Christmas Day. They were all open in the morning and a few shut for the afternoon only. On Boxing Day they all resumed normal hours with no thought of a Bank Holiday.

Back in Buenos Aires William got his baggage back practically intact. Before the arrival of his money there had been frequent ships sailing from Montevideo and Buenos Aires to Valparaiso, and he was hopeful of getting a booking soon, that route being cheaper and infinitely preferable to the Transandine railway, so he booked the only one he could find, thinking he would have a pleasant trip. Unfortunately on the day prior to sailing there was a mutiny on board and her destination was changed to Norway instead of the Falkland Islands.

Tuesday 4 January 1924. With no other ships coming in he left by train, a much less interesting way, on 4 January 1924. The Transandine journey was very dull, the train was very crowded and the track lay through dull pampa country with ordinary crops. With little to see William dozed most of the way. At Mendoza they changed into a narrow-gauge train from which point there was little cultivation. The train went into a long and slow climb through barren mountains in which the absence of snow, except on occasional peaks, combined with the long distance of visibility and absence of incident made the scenery appear less grand than expected. The longest halt was at the Incas' bridge, a natural causeway across a chasm, but there was insufficient time to view it properly. The first real panorama to be seen was near Juncal, in Chile, looking down the Aconcagua valley – the least beautiful part of his first long ride in Chile.

Comment

The outstanding features of Buenos Aires were Harrods, Calle Florida, the opera and the parks outside the town. There were a number of both cheap and moderately priced hotels in the town, but on the whole it was an expensive place in which to live. In the pursuit of overcharging Harrods seemed to reign supreme. Their policy seemed to be to maintain the most exorbitant prices for everything. Any article that failed to sell well at a fancy price was at once passed on to the subsidiary company, Gath & Chaves, who halved the price and carried on. If anything from this latter shop sold well the opposite course was adopted, and it went to Harrods who doubled the price.

The tea rooms were large and attractive and were reasonable in price. Calle Florida, the Bond Street of town, was a sort of glorified mannequin parade at certain hours of the day, when all traffic was stopped and the youth and beauty wandered up and down preening themselves and hoping to be admired by the opposite sex. The opera on the night William went was very good and the price very moderate. It was not a gala night.

Convalescence

Having reached Valparaiso William made straight for the Rest Home at Lonquen where the owners were very struck by his changed appearance and general debility. His nerves were in a dreadful state now that the strain could be relaxed and for the first few nights he upset the sleep of all the residents by letting out blood-curdling cries in his sleep. It was over a week before he was told about this so he promptly moved his bed out into a quiet corner of the garden and slept for some nights under the stars. The local watchdog, a huge mongrel, slept at the foot of William's bed, and twice during each night he used to ramble round the

park to see that all was well. On his return he invariably pushed his muzzle into William's face through the mosquito net, reporting all was safe.

One night William returned to his room because it was too wet to sleep outside. A newly-wed couple had just arrived and on the first night they failed to appear for dinner. William could not help hearing sounds as though there was trouble in the next room. Late in the evening there were sobs on the patio but he did not feel inclined to get up and console the poor damsel. Horrors when a few minutes later she appeared knocking on his door which was open. She was wearing a very fluffy and expensive dressing gown and in the bright moonlight she looked very sweet and pathetic carrying a pail. Her husband had apparently been very sick and she was unable to sleep with the pail in the room and dared not sleep with it out of the room either. In very plaintive tones she asked him if he could help. For a couple of days after William's assistance he was in great favour with this sweet girl, but when he related the story at table, he incurred the everlasting hatred of this charming young lady.

For a long time William had to take life very quietly – a trip to Valparaiso to collect more baggage from store being almost too much for his strength. He remained there for seven months as it was a suitable place to recuperate in and was near to Santiago where medical attention could be obtained if necessary.

Shortly after his return to Lonquen violent dysentery started and the only relief came from frequent doses of castor oil, so that for a long time he averaged four double doses a day. He tried doctor after doctor, each time with the same result. As soon as he started on their treatment he suffered violent intestinal pains and within a couple of days he resumed his own treatment which, if it kept him very weak, did at least keep him free from pain. He was treated for a variety of things, the malady generally being considered to be due to imagination!

There was a big turnover among the guests who came to the house for their holidays, and it was considered an ideal resort for

herds of children who stayed for weeks at a time. At an early stage during William's recovery his kit became public property as far as the children were concerned. Each time he went to the doctor he was expected to take at least one Thermos flask and to bring it back filled with ice cream for a few favoured ones.

During the hot weather a plunge bath in the garden was used a lot, no-one minding that the water was always very dirty, being surplus water from irrigating the fields. Ducking was confined to two favoured children and William – who was expected to come off worst.

One of these two children dared William to dive through the legs of a Jew staying in the house who was standing in the water with his legs well apart trying to coax one of his own kids to jump into his arms. William was halfway through before he was seen, when the Jew tried to move, consequently swallowing some water before William was able to get his head above the level of his feet again. The Jew appeared to take his ducking very well, but some time later he struck William quite hard, possibly by way of revenge.

Shooting was very popular and every time William attempted to slink out of the compound with a gun he had about a dozen followers who demanded permission to come. Many were very young children and the excursions had to be very limited in duration. From start to finish they all spoke continuously in excited whispers which were audible for hundreds of yards. Any live object was considered fair game and it was a rare event for William to get within range of anything worth shooting. Each time a bird or rabbit was seen fierce arguments started as to the course to be adopted, some urging fire at once, other to stalk up closer and others begging William not to shoot. Most of the children favoured shooting in principle, enjoying the noise of the shot, but petitions for life to be spared predominated. One day William fell into deep disgrace for shooting a young rabbit. In his death he won all their hearts, and then even those who had most urged him to shoot a few moments before turned on him for 'hitting the poor animal'. That day no more shooting was allowed and the rabbit was carried

back to the house and buried with the utmost consideration, William's suggestion that it should be eaten being vehemently turned down.

The Recovery Process

May 1924. By early May William felt well enough to think about taking a temporary job at Braden and at short notice went to see the Duke again. They met in the afternoon and had a sandwich after which they proceeded to celebrate their reunion. William had been teetotal at Lonquen but found many of the elders very trying and had become tired of the strain of continuous ultra-respectability. After a couple of drinks they walked the half-mile back to the staff house where they changed for dinner. While waiting for the meal to be served they made plans for an amusing evening, but this was interrupted when William became very dizzy for a few moments and he thought it wiser to turn in at once. He found he could not even get to his room and had to be ignominiously put to bed. He became steadily worse and had the greatest trouble in either speaking or breathing, while any light hurt his eyes and excited him. All the remedies they tried failed so by midnight they sent for a doctor who failed to make any diagnosis and after standing there for over an hour predicted his certain death before morning. William was by now feeling a little better and could hear and understand every word that he said, but his statement did not cause any additional anxiety. In the morning William was normal again and thought it prudent to return to Lonquen for a bit more rest.

About a month later he had a similar but less violent attack after drinking a single cocktail. On this occasion two ladies looked after him. While he could still stand he collected his sleeping bag and disappeared into a field of maize where they were unable to find him, and slept off the malaise. In the morning he was surprised

to find the irrigation water had been turned on during the night and the lower half of the flea-bag was under water, but luckily none came through the waterproofing or over the top.

As William became stronger the local mountain became a great attraction and he climbed it from all sides. With this experience he soon became the accredited guide for all the residents at the Rest Home. His first job was to escort an ardent boy scout and the captain of the Chilean Girl Guides, the latter claiming that she could go anywhere a man could. They took an easy route up but the descent was a short cut down a very steep and shrubby slope. The girl dislodged a small boulder accidentally and as it rolled down it caught William in the ribs and nearly knocked him out. She thought it was rather funny at the time but before the end of the outing she was extremely tired and was hardly able to move for days afterwards, so gave up talking about being able to follow a man on any track.

Despite this adventure two more children got permission to be taken up the mountain. The plan was to leave the house at dawn but at first they were too sleepy to have breakfast. It was only when William threatened not to take them that they controlled their tempers and started to get ready. On seeing how they were dressed William persuaded them to change some of their clothes, but they remained very unsuitably attired. Once started on the climb they found it much harder than expected, and thanks to the late start they thought the sun was hot. They soon took William's famous topi, and it was not long before he was carrying not only their meal to be eaten at the top, but everything else they discarded – including puttees (cloth wound round the leg from ankle to knee for protection) which were uncomfortable, and coats too hot. Not surprisingly the children blamed William when they found their stocking provided insufficient protection against the pricks of the cactus and thought it was unfair that he should wear breeches and leggings as protection against them. Anyway, they thought puttees were beastly things, and when the going got tough William was again blamed for deliberately making it hard. Eating the meal when half-way up

improved matters considerably – the children had a bit of rest and William had less to carry. They reached the summit safely and rested in some old gold workings before returning in the hottest part of the day. Once back in the house again all the pains and wailing of the morning were forgotten and they told all the others how easy it had been! This was an undoubted success, enthusiasm quickly built up and another trip was arranged to take place in a couple of days. Because all the food had to be carried by older people the meal took place more below than above a quarter of the way up. After tea a few of the more hardy people climbed another 200–300 feet, but none reached even halfway that day. Among the party on this occasion was Joyce, the youngest of the Byrne family, who became life-long friends of William and myself.

Some time later when William was visiting the Byrnes in Quilpué Joyce challenged him to go down a slide standing on a mat in skiing fashion. Within the first yard the mat stuck, and the steep slope caused William to fall forward. His first stride took him nearly halfway down, where his foot went through the slide, fortunately without being caught. Amid shrieks from the children he fell to earth rather heavily. Unfortunately he landed on his side, where he had put a bag of chocolate creams in his pocket for the younger members of the party. He suffered only a light bruise to the ribs, but his coat needed a lot of cleaning. To add to his discomfort, in an absent-minded moment he had put his tobacco pouch in the same pocket. After this neither the chocolates nor their silver paper were acceptable to any except the dog.

William went on a few riding excursions but the horses were ridden to death and gave little pleasure for hacking purposes. At first he found all the dogs in the neighbourhood were in the habit of hunting and barking at every horse that trotted or cantered along the roads. (They still do today.) As a result he took a hunting crop with him and by the time he left Lonquen the dogs left him alone.

September 1924. By September William decided to return to Valparaiso where he was told he should find better doctors. The

doctors in Santiago had failed to make any impression of a favourable sort on the aftermath of the leech, and for a long time the new doctors were no better. Dr Morgan had a good reputation and was a surgeon but William refused to go to him, fearing the worst. A mutual friend told the doctor the reason for his refusal to go, so Dr Morgan promptly admitted he would undoubtedly want to open the patient up to see the cause of the trouble. However, he also told the mutual friend that he was experimenting on some new pills which he thought might work and was prepared to guarantee that they would do no harm. In fact they were wonderful. Within a week William went to see Dr Morgan to express his thanks for the cure. The doctor confirmed that the leech was a female and all her eggs had gone down inside him. The long period of starvation had removed the gastric juices and the eggs had been occasionally hatching out.

There still remained a few more problems and this time William came under Dr Tuyl, a Dutch specialist. When he had finished with the throat problem he decided to clear an obstruction in the nose caused by an old breakage. Dr Tuyl had an enormous practice, largely among the very poorest people and he charged his clients such sums as he thought they could pay, often making no charge at all. Except for operations he never made an appointment, everyone crowding into his waiting room, and from there he drew them off into his consulting room four at a time. He may have saved a little time by this procedure but it made his patients very nervous.

William's appointment was for 10.30 a.m. and he went in with the usual group of four after a fairly long wait. After starting to inject a local anaesthetic the doctor moved on to another patient with throat trouble who, after making a number of weird noises, retired to come again another day. He gave William a few more jabs and then turned to a young flapper's eyes, but soon she left in tears. William had a few more injections and then the doctor saw the last man who by this time was on the verge of fainting from terror. After another group had passed through his hands he

finished off the patients in the waiting room and was ready to start serious operations on William.

William was seated on a stool with no back and was expected to lean forward holding a tray to catch all the blood that might flow. Gadgets were fixed to his nostrils to expand them almost to breaking point, which thanks to the cocaine he did not feel, and then he started with a knife. At first William was a bit nervous, but there was no pain except when he was extracting pieces of gristle. Late in the proceedings he was unable to cut away a piece of bone, so he went off to collect a mallet and chisel and with a few light taps cleared the obstruction, but they felt like very heavy blows. He sewed up where necessary and then came the most painful part of all. He plugged William's nose to stop the bleeding, pushing gauze right up his nostrils. The job was finished at 1.30 p.m. when he presented William with the bone he had cut away. William then retired to try and face lunch, a bad headache, and the unpleasant taste of blood.

In the afternoon the bleeding became so bad William returned to Dr Tuyl. He was delighted with his handiwork and by removing the plugging he allowed the blood to flow freely for a long time before replugging it. In spite of all that had been cut away there was no feeling of a cavity such as is felt after a tooth is extracted.

That night there was a lot more bleeding and when the maid brought his breakfast in the morning she nearly dropped the tray on seeing him. His face, throat, pillow, pyjamas, sheets, everything were covered in dried gore. Happily William did not feel too ill and for the next two days managed to carry on a quiet life. At night in particular much blood and matter went down his throat and his tongue became very swollen. By the third morning he was feeling rotten and he was also faced with a shortage of pyjamas. A little private washing had to be done and all went well until the ironing was nearly finished when the door opened – William thought he had locked it – and he jumped in front of his ironing to hide it from Byrne who was then ushered back outside, where he enquired after William's health and then quickly departed, but

not until there was a most ominous smell of burning. The next time William met the Byrne family he confessed to the laundry work and was told that Byrne was most anxious to know what garment had smelt so much when burning, but he made no offer to replace William's best silk jacket.

On the first day that William was out and about again he went to the Cancha at Viña del Mar where fishing was in progress and he watched for a while. Then at a moment when his attention was distracted elsewhere, a boy, full of hero worship, tossed a ball which landed on the point of William's still very tender nose. It was extremely painful, broke some stitches and retarded progress. William was extremely upset by this and the boy's apologies passed unheard.

A fortnight after the operation William could breathe slightly through the nose, but the scabs were painful and there was still bleeding at night. Visits to Dr Tuyl lapsed into a wait of two to three hours followed by an interview of as many minutes.

Vina del Mar Cancha, pavilion

By Armistice Day William was fairly well again. For the convenience of businessmen the 'Silence' and church service was held at noon and lasted about fifteen minutes. The church was packed full, there being about three times as many children as adults. In the evening there was an ex-servicemen's dinner. Telegrams were exchanged with Santiago, Antofagasta, Buenos Aires and other big towns where similar meals were in progress, each town stating the number of people at table.

There were about eighty people there and after a few short speeches and toasts there was a sing-song of a wartime character. Many people left early and William stayed playing bridge until the drunks got too noisy when he went to bed none the worse for having his first cocktail since the unfortunate episode at Lonquen. One or two of the senior businessmen tried to adopt a rather patronizing manner which was most noticeable in the order in which people sat down to the meal and caused some ill-feeling. At first no-one displayed their medals, but when the consul expressed a wish that they should be worn nearly everyone produced them from their pockets.

An opera company from Buenos Aires visited the town at this time and was a great success. The night William went one of the intervals became excessively long, even by South American standards. The people in the 'gods' became restive as usual until one person thought of making a paper dart and launching it out into the stalls. It floated well into the auditorium and after a very haphazard course it ended up hitting someone's bare, unsuspecting shoulders. This delighted the inventor's neighbour and they took up the idea with the greatest zest. In a short while there was a cloud of darts varying in size from a couple of inches to darts made out of double sheets of newspapers. Each was allowed to drop from the gallery, a few were thrown well out, but all were dispatched without a trace of viciousness. Great interest was shown in the course of each, while suitable squeaks were let out by ladies whenever one either hit or fell near them.

William saw a very dull combined naval and military display at

Vina del Mar cricket ground

Vina which included a sham fight done on popular lines. The navy landed field guns for both sides, and these were fired rapidly with much smoke and noise, and a complete indifference to drill and safety. They seemed to be completely unaware that guns firing shell are liable to recoil. No elevation was put on the guns which were fired into the backs of the infantry at a few yards range. In this attempt to annihilate their first-line troops they were assisted by machine-guns, and the infantry, shot at from behind, must have been glad that they were not enfiladed or chased by tanks as well. In the midst of all this smoke and confusion the Red Cross detachments of both sexes, and including at least one child of very tender years, walked about laughing and chatting with complete sang-froid and lack of sympathy for the casualties who appeared to enjoy receiving first aid. Neither the advancing waves of infantry, nor the bursts of fire, nor the applause of the spectators affected their complete self-possession.

William was known for his cricket skills in Vina del Mar and his photograph remained in the clubhouse until the building was burnt down some seventy years later.

In December 1924 people still remarked that he looked sick but it was time he left Valparaiso and he set off towards the north of Chile.

CHAPTER VI

North Chile
The Nitrate Pampa at North Lagunas

ecember 1924. Money was running out and William's journey to the north of Chile was to get work. It was now a year since he had the leech in his throat and although he was still a sick man he thought he was well enough to get back to his former work routine. His first visit was to see his old comrades at Chuquicamata and having no luck there he returned to Antofagasta. Most of the people who had offered work before had left and those that remained did not know him. It was suggested he went to Iquique and there he obtained a job at North Lagunas.

The Iquique railway was interesting in that because distances were short most people chose to travel first class so most of the carriages were first class for the locals and a special carriage at an equally special price was set apart for foreigners (*gringos*) who wished to travel in moderate comfort.

The train left half an hour late, with no reasons given, and slowly wound its way behind the town, up a hill and continued following a long valley. There was no restaurant car on the train but frequent stops at halts of a quarter of an hour gave sufficient time for refreshment. At Central the train divided into two, one portion going north and the other south. This stop was for half an hour giving passengers time for lunch at the Chinese bar.

The country was all sandy wasteland, the biggest hills were near the sea and the later undulations were very small. In the afternoon

a hot wind blew up so much dust the carriage windows had to be closed making it very stuffy.

The train was only an hour late when it reached its final destination, shortly after sundown, an early arrival for this particular train. The manager of the company's wife and mother-in-law were also on the train so there was no delay in being met and William joined them to be taken to the staff quarters, a single-storey wooden building divided into two, one for the manager and the other for the remainder of the staff. The difference in comfort was very striking, the manager having almost luxurious fittings.

The staff had nothing in particular to grumble at. The food was good but not pretentious. Only water was allowed at meal times and was very salty. This upset newcomers at first but they became used to it. All staff quarters had become teetotal now because of the recent fall in profits, but some individuals were able to have private supplies sent up from Iquique.

The rooms were sparingly furnished and the furniture had seen better days. All the rooms opened into a central hall which was covered with Guayquil cane which kept the hall cool and dark enough to be free of flies. In the centre of the hall the manager kept a supply of quail and doves in a large cage for special occasions. All the windows were heavily barred for protection in times of riots.

The billiard room was next to the dining room and the resident engineer had recently recovered the table. There was a sitting room with papers mostly many months old. The pianola and gramophone had been recently removed by the manager on his marriage, but he left the pianola music open for staff to see, although it was doubtful if it was ever played. The bathroom and toilet were the only badly ventilated and smelly parts of the whole building.

The manager's dining room was his most ambitious effort – strikingly black with imitation panelling on the bottom of the walls and a white ceiling, but he did not have a polished table to show it off.

Outside the manager's part of the house there was a tennis court

which was surprisingly good to play on. Usually staff could only find time to play in the evening when the sun shone straight down the court. Otherwise it was mostly used as a yard to exercise the manager's puppies and suffered from the resultant mess.

Next to this was a very fertile garden of about 15 square yards, for which all the soil had to be brought up from many miles away.

The workmen's dwellings consisted of a miserable collection of hovels behind the staff house. Each man was given two nominal rooms to furnish as he liked and which, in consequence, were usually bare. At the back of each quarter there was a small yard in which a kitchen was made by means of a couple of stolen sheets of corrugated iron. All the older huts had walls of corrugated iron which were very hot, but recently it had been found more economic and better to use sun-dried mud bricks.

The YMCA building was in the centre of the camp and twice a week it was used as a cinema.

The *pulperia*, a dry-store canteen, was maintained to sell goods as cheaply as possible and officially it barely covered it's cost. It was run by an old Polish chess master with whom William spent many evenings and improved his game considerably.

The Chilean ideas on sanitation left much to be desired. Latrines were built but had never been used. The outskirts of the camp were very dirty and flies abounded but strangely there was almost complete immunity from epidemics of any sort, the sick list being composed almost entirely of accidents through mishandling explosives. The reason for this was given as the dryness of the air, the heat of the sun and the large numbers of scavenging birds that collected round the camp and which were almost tame.

The staff house was connected to the company offices by a short corridor which was convenient as much work was done after dinner in the evenings. William's work was to be in the laboratory which was situated a few yards beyond the accountant's office and, having recently been done up, it attracted many flies. It was well fitted out with essential equipment for the normal running of the works.

There was a lot of material for research work which had been

neglected and few of the bottles had any labels. It took some weeks to sort these out and even longer to get curtains to darken the room to remove the flies. Formalin proved useful to kill the flies slowly, and small mice came to eat the dead. Later William succeeded in intercepting a Flit sprayer which was sent up from Iquique for the manager's wife, and this made working conditions much more comfortable. Fleas cannot survive on the pampa and although the train coming up from Iquique might be alive with them when it returned the following morning they would all be dead.

Beyond the offices there was the whole of the plant for the manufacture of nitrate of soda and beyond that were a few better huts for the senior labourers.

The name Lagunas is deceptive as there is no water for miles around, the ground being very flat with nothing but sun-baked hard sand in every direction. The nearest oasis was about 20 miles away and the company's water supply was brought up from there in pipes. Other oases further north supplied a little of the food required for the pampa, the remainder being brought up from the south in coastal ships and then by the nitrate railway from Iquique.

The whole area was pitted with craters from 3 to 7 feet deep, their edges overlapping making it hard to move across country except by recognized tracks.

The narrow prospecting boreholes seemed to be put down very haphazardly and when sufficiently good values were found the holes were opened out and a charge of gunpowder, made from dirty nitrate mixed with coal dust, was dropped in and fired.

There was a barren hill between North and Central Lagunas, a slight rise 2 miles to the east and a few high hills about 6 miles to the west. In the lowest areas the standing water level was only a few feet below the surface, the water being very saline. So much so that nearby a small company made pure common salt by sinking small pits and allowing evaporation to dry up the water and the salt to solidify and seal the ground against damp. As soon as the salt had been put in bags the water bubbled up from below again and the process was repeated.

Reconstruction of crushing plant and carrier belt

The only trace of vegetation outside the garden was a mile away where there was a leak in the water pipe and where the water had washed all the salt out of the ground for a square yard or so.

The nearest neighbour was at Central Lagunas which lay about a mile away over a small hill, and a mile and a half beyond that was South Lagunas, the third of the group of mines/offices (locally referred to as *oficinas*). All three *oficinas* were very old and were considered to be nearly worked out.

Each *oficina* was served by a small railway. North Langunas had three railways and when necessary other branch lines were laid to convenient points, possibly for only a few journeys where in shallow ground nitrate values were poor but iodine and potassium salts were high. The shallowness of the ground caused the surface to be traversed quickly so it was not economical to load the 'costra' into carts and pay for extra handling.

Part of the process of the nitrate was crushing lumps about 10 inches in diameter to pass through a 2-inch mesh. A conveyor belt took it to bins where it was classified into three grades, and then fed into tanks for boiling. The tanks were filled with water (costing a farthing per gallon– .104 new pence) and the water was heated

Reconstruction of carrier belt

by the steam pipes that lined each tank. The behaviour of the water at varying temperatures was interesting, common salt being picked up, held at low temperatures and dropped in favour of nitrates at the higher ones.

The iodine house had to be particularly well ventilated and well guarded as this commodity was highly profitable for thieves. The iodine was cut in a big wooden tank with either sulphuric acid and hypo or with carbonate of soda made by burning dirty nitrate and coal dust in an open pit. The metallic iodine floated to the surface and was filtered off in an old coarse sack. During the cutting and filtering process the vapour got so dense that a number of workmen were blinded for several days.

William arrived during a period of reconstruction and a new conveyor belt (the longest on the nitrate pampa) and crushing plant were being erected. A new labour force was brought up from the agricultural districts of Chile and when work recommenced there were 500 men on the payroll. This number fluctuated each week, as most of them moved a few miles away to the next mine, so for this reason the companies took it in turns to import the labour from the south.

Arrangements made for the comfort of the men arriving was disgraceful and if large numbers of animals had been treated in the same way they would have died. The men were herded together in trucks without food or water, shunted about unnecessarily, and arriving at Lagunas late at night, they were kept there until the following morning. None had a penny to their name, no change of clothing, and their only baggage was their bedding. They seemed more suitably dressed for the Arctic than for the tropics, claiming they were keeping the rays of the sun off them. It was a marvel they did any work at all dressed as they were. The plant ran for twenty-four hours a day in regular shifts, the men having no fixed hours but generally starting work in the dark and going on until nearly midday. They returned to camp for a siesta and did another couple of hours work at the end of the afternoon.

In early March 1925, shortly after the reopening of the mine,

there was some rain, the first for seven years. It was little more than a light Scotch mist but there it was considered heavy. It came through the more or less open roofs washing in dust that had settled on top which stained everything it came in contact with; it also reduced the number of flies around. In the mountains the rains were severe and washed away a number of bridges on the railway line resulting in a shortage of food on the pampa.

It was customary for all managers to keep a reserve of nitrate in case of a bad month's output so as to maintain an even cost of production. Some *oficinas* claimed the rain had washed a lot of nitrate off the drying grounds (*canchos*), which excuse they undoubtedly used to replenish their private supplies.

In the early days William went through some rather painful learning experiences. He frequently hit his fingers with a hammer when testing samples, spilled acid over himself in the laboratory and on one occasion fell among beams when attempting to jump a big open pit during reconstruction. The worst disaster was in the laboratory when he was distracted while sucking up sulphuric acid in a pipette and he drew in a complete mouthful, luckily not swallowing any, but it removed all the skin from his lips and mouth. It was very painful for days afterwards and he spent much time gargling various soothing liquids. The labourers played tricks on him by salting their samples and watching the results with interest.

After a time William suffered from a number of boils and one of these on his chest turned into an abscess. The doctor was unable to get rid of it so William tried a mustard plaster. Mustard, boiling water, bread and all the rags that might be required were obtained and as soon as William was in his pyjamas and lying helpless on his back Green, the engineer, assisted. After a preliminary scalding he applied the mustard to the boil in a handkerchief. As it was dry he then swilled water all over William, swamping the bed and the floor, washing away all the mustard and reducing the mattress to a sticky yellow pulp in parts. He was delighted with his success and left William for a few minutes to collect some more mustard

and water – he was not going to make the mistake of washing away all the mustard this time. Mustard, mustard and still more mustard was added to the rags on William's chest and more boiling water was used causing more scalds, after which William was covered up with every available blanket, rug and carpet to keep the heat in. The mustard drew out the matter and William's whole body was stinging. When he could stand it no longer he kicked off all the coverings and applied a bread poultice in its place which proved very soothing. He had a bad night's sleep and in the daylight of the following morning he could see mustard all over the place. Skin was missing from all sorts of unlikely places considering the boil was on his chest. There were raw patches of flesh under one armpit, in the small of his back, on one thigh and various other places. His 'blessings' flowed freely on Green who accepted them smilingly and almost with pride. That afternoon he attempted to play tennis with Comber who was suffering from a stiff back. Neither could pick up the balls with any ease and soon they both had to give up.

Late in March 1925, after much persistent asking, William got permission to ride over to the company wells and pumping plant one Sunday morning. He started at 6.00 a.m. on a rotten horse. For the first hour there was a raw mist and a nip in the air which enlivened the horse who went quite well for the first few miles, but it was so cold William could hardly hold the reins. The track was well marked between pipes and telephone lines and after 7 miles in a northerly direction came a long slope to the north-east. It was too steep and sandy to move faster than a walk and the horse thought he was tired. Not a vestige of green could be seen anywhere, outcrops of rock being the only variation from never-ending sand. At the end of a 5- or 6-mile climb came a sharp descent of about a mile where the pumping station could be seen about 5 miles away. The road for the last part was good and very hard.

The man in charge was an Irishman who had married a Chilean farming woman. They seemed to have numerous children and lived

in a typical corrugated-iron type of house which was very dirty. Few people were allowed to enter and those who did would not wish to enter a second time. There was a little oasis and a small very green patch of garden. He was almost illiterate and had lived there for twenty years doing the same job – small wonder he had few topics of conversation. Once a month he went to the *oficina* to draw his pay and purchase a little beer.

By special permission of the manager a chicken was slain for William's lunch which was eaten outside under the shade of a large tree. The chicken was hashed up in some way and William found it surprising how many legs it had and the apparent absence of a body.

The wells were about 150 feet deep and when full contained about 15 feet of water. Their capacity was unknown due to their liability to cave in. All the pumping was done by motors which drove the water to the main pumping plant, from where it was lifted to the top of the hill William had just climbed, and then it ran down by gravity to the *oficinas*.

The return journey was delayed for an hour due to the disappearance of William's saddle. It was the hottest time of the day so William took a longer route avoiding the big climb. In one place where there was water on the surface the steam could be seen from a long distance off.

Although moving at a slow walk William and his horse were both in a muck sweat. He called in at Bellavista *oficina* to see the rugger ground that had been prepared for the match in early May between the Port and Pampa teams. It was well rolled and not a stone to be seen, but it was heavy underfoot and looked as if it might be very dusty in play.

April 1925. William was detailed to meet and look after a young lad who was the son of a director of many companies. He already had the reputation of being 'rather a foul affair'. According to custom, en route to meet him William dropped in to nets at Central Lagunas, and from there periodically rang up the station

to find out where the train was. During an animated discussion the train was forgotten until they heard it arriving at the station something over a mile distant. When nearing the station the manager's trolley came rushing down the slope on the rails, but out of control and with the embryo director in it. William rushed back after him hailing lustily as the trolley came to rest about a mile down the track where he joined the boy. After a pause to regain his breath he welcomed the lad and was promptly asked why the manager had not come in person to meet him. He then spoke about all the important positions held by his father who was about to retire from some of them and put this 'wart' in his place. William was duly impressed and the lad then talked about various other subjects, especially about the Army, and before reaching the *oficina* William felt bound to shut him up very decisively.

Slightly hurt by this he had a further shock when he found that not only was the manager not there waiting to meet him, he had not been invited to stay in his part of the house either.

William reported the arrival to Comber and gave a quick resumé of the trip in the trolley. Very definite orders were promptly given that under no circumstances was he to be allowed to go to the manager's rooms. William had to take the uninvited guest to dinner and as they entered the dining room the remainder of the staff, who had almost finished their meal, were introduced and then walked out of the room.

The meal was not very good and William had to look after him that evening and the following morning when he was to be shown round the property, but was not to interfere in any degree with normal work. The lad informed William that he knew all that there was to be known about the industry and aired much of his knowledge. William felt obliged to put him in his place, his information being more exclusive and of a nature that would have appalled anyone who knew even a little about the subject. The boy was very gullible and grateful and confidentially told William that people at the last place he went to had dared to try and pull his leg, but he was too clever for them, confident that he could

Filling cachuehos with caliche

pull his weight on any boards he sat on. William duly allowed him to show his worth by testing '*caliche*' in the proper pampa manner with a hammer and wick, and in a few minutes he was proving to his own satisfaction that salt was nitrate. As a result of this, before leaving he complimented Comber on his reserve grounds. Comber was mystified until William explained the error. William never heard the results of his passing on what he had 'learnt' while there.

Soon after this event the manager's wife had her first baby. It was much overdue and when the time came she kept everyone awake with her screams that sounded hardly allied to either pain or fear and the staff felt little sympathy for her. For the superstitious the omens were not good. Just before and after the event there were earthquakes, the night was very dark and gloom fell over the place until midday. There was a railway strike on and rumours of yet another coup d'état in Santiago with other disturbances closer at hand. There seemed to be no star to shine on the child.

Comment

William remained almost teetotal while there and found it most trying sitting down to dinner while often four out of the six were drunk or nearly so. His tact on such occasions was not obvious but his need to be friends with them was not necessary either as he had plenty of work to do at the *oficina* and he also assisted the research chemists with data, spending much time reading up their past work. For recreation he played tennis with Comber and others. Hunt, the manager at Central, was a great sportsman who maintained the cricket ground and golf links. If cricket could not be readily arranged, he had nets up most evenings and detailed all his staff as well as himself to turn out for a couple of hours' practise. While William was there they played three matches, in the last of which Hunt and William damaged their knees which kept them hobbling for the next few weeks.

The Communist Rising, June 1925

Communist agitators became more active after the railway strike and it became known that early in June they intended giving a further display of their power, probably in the form of another railway strike of even a general strike.

In the first days of the month the leaders of the party from all *oficinas* went to Iquique to attend a series of secret meetings. On the first Friday it was heard that some official action had been taken against them and the meeting was broken up – the senior officials being shipped off on a cruiser to Juan Fernandez, two days' sail from Iquique. The Communists were furious and early next morning many of them forcibly took over the working of a number of *oficinas*. In each case the staff were caught totally unprepared as they had not expected this form of trouble and they handed the keys over without a struggle. The Communists killed

the *carabineros* (police) out of hand and mutilated their bodies. In two cases the staff had sufficient warning and defended themselves with rifles, inflicting heavy casualties on their assailants.

As each *oficina* was taken over a Communist was immediately established to take charge of everything. The plant was supposed to be kept running and all profits were to be distributed among the labourers. Office staff got nothing, but there was no looting of buildings or kits of the deposed staff.

At 5.30 p.m. one afternoon the *jefe-de-pampa* came in from the pampa to inform Comber that he had firm evidence that the three *oficinas* in the group would be attacked that evening soon after the arrival of the train from Inquique. The local leaders were returning on the same train and would be in time to take up their positions. In the event of their non-arrival the show was to start at once without them.

There were insufficient *oficina* staff to deal with the situation unaided and they were further handicapped by having two women present. The staff house could not be defended, being highly inflammable and the whole of the back part could be reached without being observed from within. It was important to establish what the staff proposed doing. Nearly all wanted to leave but Shepherd was anxious to become a warrior again, while Comber gave nothing away, so William had a chat with him. They realized that Comber would be the man they would kill first and he had everything to gain by defending himself. At the end of a stormy interview he handed over all his carbines (short rifles used by cavalry) and ammunition to William to keep in his room as it was the most central position of defence. The Communists had omitted to cut the telephone lines so Comber sent an SOS to the police headquarters at Alianza and a patrol was sent to their assistance immediately. They had a long ride before them and could not be expected to arrive until after dark. Furthermore it was probable that the line had been tapped and the attack would be precipitated.

The wait from dusk until dinner was not pleasant. For greater security in the dark William loaded his shotgun as being more

serviceable than a carbine. The building was shut up, no-one was allowed out for a walk and no arms were to be seen anywhere. Meanwhile William, Comber and Shepherd, bristling with pistols in every pocket, wandered about aimlessly.

Dinner was very quiet and William came under a cloud for casually remarking that although he knew none of them would do so, he would have much pleasure in shooting the first person he saw deserting. Most of the men had already made plans for getting away quickly and took these remarks personally. None confessed they had no intention of putting up a show, while to be ushered into William's room and then be caught with arms in their hands after firing had started would be signing their death warrants if captured.

Before they had finished their soup Comber was noticed passing the door, going towards the office. A moment later Mrs Comber, very white and palpitating, appeared to say that there was a group of men at the front door asking for him. Unintentionally the sound of a war-whoop slipped out and before William had reached the door all the staff, with the exception of Shepherd who continued eating his soup, had disappeared and were not seen again until the following morning.

Mrs Comber told William to follow her to the best vantage point to see who the men were. As he reached the window she switched on the light leaving him beautifully illuminated, so William hastily turned the light off. Not seeing anyone there she proposed taking William to her bedroom, but he saw no object in going there and declined. At that moment she saw and identified her crowds – it was the night-watchman alone and he had come round to report that the patrol had arrived. On hearing the news she almost broke down. Comber was quickly found, billets fixed up, a guard posted at North Lagunas and the remainder went to the other *oficinas*, carefully going among the huts to ensure that all knew that they were present. They finally returned and settled down at North Lagunas for the night. William sat by the telephone throughout the night in case of trouble, feeling tired and nervous.

After some time a loud noise suddenly aroused him, and ready to defend himself he cautiously went towards the source of it only to find that an extra night watchman had been put on guard duty and he had tripped over his dog.

By Sunday morning news was coming in from other districts, so William wandered over to Central for nets as usual only to find the staff still standing there, ready to shoot.

On Monday it was back to work so William went out on to the pampa early and came across no unpleasantness but noticed that many men were absent. Returning to the camp at midday he was struck by the businesslike air of the troops. They had just completed a search for arms and for the ringleaders of the district, rounding up about a dozen whose names had been obtained from the Bolshies' own records of their order of seniority and activity. The official Communist papers gave much enlightening information.

During the afternoon the prisoners were marched off under mounted escort but before reaching the next *oficina* all were said to have attempted to escape and paid the usual penalty. Their widows and families were sent off to Inquique the next morning to be shipped to the south again.

Comment

William left the Lagunas and later heard that the Communists had nearly succeeded. The *Intendente* (chief of police) had got wind of the trouble only just in time and wired for more troops to be sent at once from Tacna. At the same time he arrested the ringleaders which upset their plans for a united rising, for whereas all *oficinas* should have risen at the same time many started operations some hours too early while many failed at act at all. After the first mutilations were known, the *carabineeros* (police) were ready to defend themselves to the last, while a patrol raided the Iquique train and caught most of the delegates carrying their orders with them, thus leaving the rank and file of Bolshevism without leaders

or orders but with a threat of trouble if they stirred. They sat still and did nothing.

To suppress the districts that had achieved some measure of success cavalry, artillery and infantry were rushed on to the pampa. In three *oficinas* there were pitched battles fought in the style of glorified field days with moving but helpless targets. An artillery bombardment preceded an infantry attack, supported by machine-gun fire, the attack being driven home with a cavalry charge. Most of the leaders captured in Inquique were taken to sea in a cruiser and made to walk the plank in the old-fashioned manner, leaving no traces behind. Officially casualties were said to have been about a hundred, but the figure generally accepted was 3,000-4,000, which included all the prisoners who tried to escape either on foot or by swimming the Pacific.

Las Chiles Copper Mine

August 1925. William paid a visit to Las Chiles copper mine in August 1925, accompanied by an expert chemist from the research department. There were said to be good profits there but the Americans who were working it ran out of money and had to close it down.

The entrance was in the hills 6 miles away from the *oficina*. The wind at the top of the hill was so strong the horses could hardly stand up against it and so the men dismounted and went on foot by a covered way to the main shaft. On a previous visit William noted the ladders were still in position although the mine was deserted; there was a long steel cable hanging down which he would use if the ladders were unsafe and he brought a pair of thick gloves to save his hands from being too badly cut. There was no way his companion was going down that shaft but he would get help if William got stuck.

The first 50 or 60 feet were easy, the daylight was good and the

ladders sound. From here there were two shafts down about a hundred feet apart. One shaft was short and uninteresting, the other was fairly deep and there were already plenty of traces of copper. It was now totally dark and the ladders had many rungs missing. It went to a total depth of about 500 feet, the bottom 50 feet being down inclined poles, each about 6 inches wide and notched on one side. There was no ventilation and every few feet William struck matches to ensure the air was sufficiently pure for breathing as it was stifling and by now he was in a muck sweat. He remained at the bottom only a few minutes before coming up again at a much faster pace than the descent. It took an hour altogether and at the top found the air felt quite cold so that he was shivering even when sitting in the sun and out of the wind.

Having now resigned from North Lagunas William stayed on to see the Chilean Independence Day festival on 18 September (Diez-y-ocho). This is always a day of great celebration and is a national holiday. It was said to be celebrated with more zest on the nitrate pampas than anywhere else and after the recent uprising it was expected there would be an even greater display of national patriotism.

The first official event was at noon on 17 September when a band, costing the equivalent of fifty pounds sterling, played the National Anthem. At the same time a salute of twenty-one minute guns was fired, represented by sticks of dynamite being let off at minute intervals outside the offices.

For weeks before the event the men had saved every penny they could for this fiesta and by the 16th all the labour, except for two old Bolivians, had disappeared. By noon the only men left were those around the office trying to get more pay or borrow more money. The playing of the anthem and firing of guns continued all day and by the 17th they were all well and truly drunk – and were only able to move when a stick of dynamite accidentally fell near their feet. As cash and sobriety departed, so patriotism and salutes waned. William added to the general gaiety by planting booby-trap landmines of potassium perchlorate (or the old iodine)

and ammonia, spreading machinations where the salutes were fired. The drunks were quite unable to account for the explosions under their feet and a few sobered up quite quickly. There were no accidents.

On the evening of 18 September there was a great dance given by the YMCA which lasted until midday on the 19th. The younger members of staff attended and were much the worse for wear for many days afterwards. All the drinks were illicit which reduced the supply and enhanced the price, and by the 19th the place had been drunk dry and all the money spent.

The excitement of the fiesta was over and William, feeling rather bored, visited the other two *oficinas* but they were also in a state of torpor. Mounted sports were taking place in each case, but there was no interest in the events except that every time the referee made a decision he was fiercely challenged. William ended the day at the nets, still badly handicapped by the injured knee from the Port v. Pampa match.

Casualties were not infrequent during these fiestas. Two years previously there was a Mr X of South Lagunas who was famous for his quarrelsome disposition. On this particular occasion he relaxed and, gathering his chief enemies together, proposed that all should for once drink to their great nation at his expense. He shook each warmly by the hand. They were dumbfounded at this unexpected prodigality but the offer was one they could not refuse. While they stood in a group round him he produced half a dozen bottles of beer from his pockets and handed them round. This munificence aroused considerable suspicion, but even that died away when he allowed one of the others to change bottles with him and, opening it with 'Salut' and 'Viva Chile' he tossed off the contents. Suspicion over, his newly-made friends soon had their eyes fixed on the tipped-up ends of their bottles – a quick deft sweep of a knife reduced the population of the pampa by four, after which the supplier of the drinks wiped the blood off his weapon, cursed his fallen victims and cleared off safely. Such was the danger of drinking beer.

CHAPTER VII

Bolivia

La Paz and Lake Titicaca

t the end of September 1925 William left the nitrate pampa in search of better things in Bolivia. He had to wait two days at Arica for the weekly train to La Paz and spent this time mostly in Tacna. Both towns were crowded with people imported from Peru and Chile to ensure ample votes in the plebiscite that had been ordained by the American commission which was nominally settling the dispute

The Lecture

Parade celebrating the Battle of Tacna

between the two countries. Prices had risen sharply, and the Vergara Hotel was now charging two pounds a night for a single room without meals.

There had been a number of minor riots as both countries ran local papers devoted to abusing the other side, and on every occasion when the arbitrators gave a decision the losing side took

Oruro

Tupiza valley showing Colquechaca

the opportunity of accusing them of being unduly partisan or of having succumbed to bribes. Twice the Tacna-Arica train was wrecked when carrying Peruvian voters to Tacna and each time it was proved to the satisfaction of all good Chileans that the deed had been provoked and was well merited. Feelings ran high and both sides were always anxious to urge the others to excesses out of which they could manufacture propaganda.

The cavalry officers William had met who had taken part in the suppression of the Bolsheviks on the nitrate pampa were unanimous in their joy at having had such an opportunity of displaying their military prowess.

Tacna was a beautiful green haven after the barrenness of the pampa and the thoughts of moving on saddened William, but he had to catch the Monday evening train from Arica to La Paz. The climb to high altitudes was said to be very quick and altitude sickness had to be avoided somehow, so he went to bed very early after taking copious draughts of Enos. He slept well and had no problems until the following morning when at a height of about 14,000 feet he felt sick. Up to about 14,500 feet there was a steady climb, after which there was a slight drop.

From daylight until approaching La Paz the scenery was very

Typical laundry scene on all streams near La Paz

dull, the sandy pampa having a slightly greenish tinge all the time, and the hills were insufficiently abrupt to be interesting or scenic. There were occasional flocks of llamas either grazing or carrying burdens, a few groups of Indian huts and farmhouses (*haciendas*), but no towns or villages, just vast open spaces.

The customs officers at Charana were easily satisfied but by the time the train reached Viacha, William was distinctly bored. Here

South of La Paz

the train divided, one portion going south or Oruro and the other to La Paz, with a connecting train to Lake Titicaca.

At Viacha there were a number of huts for the railway employees and a few native huts. It was not a town and there was no hotel or restaurant of any sort.

The scenery continued to be very dull until the final downhill stretch into La Paz where some of the views were the finest William had ever seen. Behind was an almost perfect horizontal skyline, and in front a deep valley into which the train descended, winding in and out of the hillside. The sandstone cliffs were worn away in a similar manner to those in Tupiza, though not quite to the same degree.

On the far side of the valley a number of peaks in the Andes were clearly visible, many covered with snow and glaciers, while towering above all was Illimani, one of the giants of South America. The colours varied greatly from pure snow white to muddy whites and browns, and bright greens to reds of all shades, while above was a cloudless bright blue sky. When the train had descended nearly a thousand feet La Paz could be seen for the first time, lying near the head of the valley down a very steep slope some 1,500 feet below. With the possible exception of Llasa, this must be a unique sight. At frequent intervals the train crossed small trickles of water and in each there were a number of Bolivian women doing their washing, the bright colours of their clothing spread out on the ground adding to the picturesque views. The women wore many layers of skirts and William found they took great pride in washing the outside layers, but thought they never washed themselves.

La Paz

The town was intended to be built on the American block system, but the steep hills nullified the results. The main streets ran steeply

La Paz

up the slopes of the valley, away from the river in the town centre where it was roughly 20 feet wide. Some of the roads were almost too steep for even good cars to climb in safety, while the tramlines zigzagged round as best they could to give the cars a chance to circulate round the town. The streets and pavements were narrow and cobbled. The shops were very poor, even in comparison to Iquique, and there was no attempt at good window dressing. Prices were very high, even for the simplest things, for example, twenty-five envelopes cost six shillings (30 new pence), the price having been marked on the box before they saw the visitor coming. The better shops were scattered about near the main plaza and there was not much to choose between them in prices.

The number of cars in the town was enormous, especially those belonging to government officials. Each of these officials seemed to be supplied with several cars which they used to take out their various wives and concubines at public expense.

Troops returning from a route march in La Paz

The most outstanding feature of the town was undoubtedly the large number of Indian women carrying babies on their backs. They were carried until they were about six years old, and up to that age they were generally incapable of feeding themselves. Glancing through the deaths reported in the La Paz newspapers William observed that the number of infants who died under three was over ten times that of the remainder mentioned.

All the women were extraordinarily industrious, and rarely did William see one walking along the roads or country tracks who was not spinning as she walked. Usually they carried a baby on their backs or some package in a shawl slung across the shoulders. The older women all wore national costume consisting of a white, very high-crowned straw hat, a short blouse and then umpteen layers of very brightly coloured skirts. These were of light material, fairly tight fitting at the waist, but the lower portion was full, heavy and thick. According to repute the women always put a new skirt on top of the remainder and allowed the older ones to gradually rot off. William witnessed six or seven outside layers coming off without making any appreciable difference to the bulk of those worn, and there was no apparent difference between the one that was on view when fully dressed and those immediately below and out of public view.

In strong contrast, their daughters usually dressed in European style and in the towns they never seemed to do any work. The same description applied forty years later to women living in and around Cuzco, Peru, where the children wore school uniform, which detracted greatly from the scenic beauty of the Andes and the rich colours of the national costume.

William arrived shortly after the centenary celebrations of Bolivia becoming a republic. There had been a great burst of enthusiasm in public works and the town was throbbing with activity. Most of the street beggars had been called in to the local labour schemes and everywhere they were either building or destroying something. William did not see any recently completed project but thought that might have been looking too closely at unimportant details.

Accommodation was found at a pension for English-speaking people run by Mrs Murray, a middle-aged English lady. It was neither expensive nor select but William found a good friend in the Peruvian chess champion with whom he had some excellent games of chess and improved his game considerably. Having recently received instruction from the Polish Master at Lagunas (whose game was far superior) he was now at his best enabling him to win two games in 200 and he managed to draw six of the remainder.

The other residents were mostly women who William only met at meal times and that was more than enough. They sat at one long table presided over by Mrs Murray. Each request of these women was advertised by screams at the servants combined with tugging at their skirts, no matter if the servant was waiting on someone else at the time. The first time William observed this behaviour it caused a dish of vegetables to fall into another lady's lap.

Shortages in knives, forks and spoons were remedied by the residents taking the nearest available dirty ones from a plate and wiping them on a table cloth, napkin or skirt – or even leaving them dirty. Once the servants left the room for any reason it was hard to get them back and Mrs Murray at frequent intervals would go berserk on a small bell, hammering it and drowning all conversation until the servants returned. These interruptions lasted for anything up to ten minutes, after which conversation resumed as though nothing had happened. The subjects discussed were either about ailments or the mysterious workings of the tummy.

The servants adopted similar remedies to the residents in cases of shortages of plates and bowls. On one such occasion the contents of the bread plate were tipped onto the floor and the plate wiped on a very dirty skirt behind Mrs Murray's back, after which it was handed to her to receive a helping of pudding. William was always served early and therefore had no reason to fear the extra rapid washing procedure. Because of a shortage of plates he took the opportunity to go into the kitchen which he found surprisingly clean.

The police in the town had the usual South American habit of blowing their whistles every quarter of an hour during the night to show that they had not left their posts. They seemed to have a system of communicating all was well by starting whistles in one corner of town followed by others in turn until all the town had been covered. These calls took place at regular intervals so it was not uncommon to see a policeman drinking with friends, and then breaking off their conversation to go to his post in time for his next whistle.

The police appeared to be very polite when making arrests. On one occasion two of them arrested a very drunk labourer. For some minutes they discussed the advisability or otherwise of the arrest being made, but the drunken man was lacking in the essentials of ordinary politeness and suddenly spat directly at one of the policemen and ran off. The two constables looked at each other sorrowfully, shrugged their shoulders and departed looking somewhat depressed.

William explored the locality and took several walks down the valley. For nearly 3 miles the road was good and trams were used for public transport. Thereafter the road became a sandy track which further along was covered in a thick layer of dust. On one walk along the side of the valley his intention was to return by tram for the last part through the town. Having descended some way down the valley William found himself walking along the bed of a small creek to avoid any climbing on his way down to the bottom of the valley. The ravine dropped increasingly below ground level and the cliffs were too steep to climb. He did not want to retrace his footsteps so continued for almost 2 miles by which time he had to clamber and slither through a number of most unpleasant water-worn tunnels which worsened as he approached the bottom of the valley. In many places there had been recent slides of earth. By now it was too late to attempt to return and singularly difficult to advance. As he came out of the last tunnel he saw another vertical cliff 300 feet high above him and the water at the foot of the hill was so close that there was no choice but to cross it or

return the way he had come. After several futile attempts to cross by means of stepping stones he then attempted (unsuccessfully) to jump from one stone to another and discovered the water was several feet deep in the middle. He was soaked through and when he reached the tram people could not understand why he was so wet as it had not been raining, but it was important to get back quickly for the nights got cold very soon after sundown and William was in urgent need of a bath and change of clothes.

The Centenary Exhibition contained a wonderful display of all the minerals to be found in the country. Indian fancy dresses were quaint or gruesome and the pickled mummies quite revolting. Half the country's imports were various brands of whisky and they were given as much space as all the other imported goods put together. There was even one brand of whisky called 'Scotch' which was made in Chile!

In the museum in La Paz were some pre-Inca idols which were similar to the early Egyptian ones. The stone was soft to touch but must have contained some tough properties enabling it to last so long. William brought some examples of these home and displayed them on the drawing-room mantlepiece.

The curator told William about a trip to Cochabamba and then to the mouth of the Amazon by a regular service of boats and trains for only forty pounds. The whole journey only required a week on mule-back and sounded interesting.

The day after arriving in La Paz William met Smith, General Manager of the Fabulosa Mines, who was looking for staff prior to taking over the properties for an English company, and William was offered a job. While awaiting his start date he worked in Barrende Hesse's laboratory and at the end of the week Smith told William to accompany him the following weekend. The night before they were due to leave they heard the properties had been taken over by fully armed men accompanied by soldiers, so William was given paid leave until it was safe to go to the mines. The British chargé d'affaires did all he could to recover the property but after a fortnight it was clear it was a case of lengthy litigation,

which took five months to recover the property and a further two months of legal troubles.

William disliked receiving a retaining fee for doing nothing and decided to go on a trip to Lake Titicaca, but kept in touch with Smith for work in the future.

Lake Titicaca

William had many problems leaving Mrs Murray's pension. The bill was not ready, although it had been requested the previous day, and the porter either could not or would not find a taxi, so William got one for himself. The same porter also decided he was incapable of carrying William's luggage down to the taxi. Mrs Murray told him to settle up on his return.

At the station he left most of his luggage in the cloak room, and taking very little with him found a seat in a very crowded train, thanks mainly to a railway porter.

The route out of La Paz was slightly different from that of his arrival and climbed to a much greater height above the town before losing sight of it, the scenery being even more arresting than when

Guaqui, Lake Titicaca, Bolivia

he arrived. On the top of the plateau the land was very barren and uninteresting and remained so until more than halfway to the lake after which it improved slowly. On the way the train passed Tiahuanaco where the pre-Inca ruins are even better than at Cuzco but there was no hostel there so William went on to Guaqui from where he would sail. There he had a most imposing reception as the railway staff had wired ahead and arranged for him to be met and escorted on board the ship. After settling down on board ship there were several hours to spare before sailing so William had a good walk round the village. It was a very dirty, smelly, straggling garrison town for a cavalry regiment, similar to the Near East. All the children in the town and for a long way around displayed extreme terror on seeing any man. Even if the man was a hundred yards away they rushed to their mothers and never left them again until the man was out of sight. This situation appeared in other places, but never so much as here where the soldiers had a bad reputation.

Outside the town and in the country districts the children were put to work almost before they could walk. They were carried to the edge of where the parents were farming and there they were dumped in charge of pigs, sheep or other farm animals. Those that could walk followed their parents in single file although the tracks were broad.

Near the borders of the lake there were many efforts to cultivate the land and even to grow trees. The edge of the lake was a grazing area, the reeds in the water being considered very good food for cattle, sheep and pigs which wallowed in it up to their bellies. The only method of moving the livestock out of the water was by throwing clods of earth and shouting vigorously, often being totally ineffective. At one port they had tried using slings to catch the animals but although they had considerable practice their results were poor.

William's first feelings on seeing the lake were of surprised delight. It was a tremendous size and perfectly beautiful, the nearest islands closing in the Guaqui end were some miles away. The

Balsas at dawn

surrounding hills were rocky and barren, sloping down to a wide beach and slowly deepening water with a long fringe of rushes and various water weeds. The water was a very bright blue, with a *balsa* (raft) here and there sailing in to land. The *balsas* were heavy canoes built of reeds woven together, each about 12 feet long and 4 feet wide. The sails were also made from reeds and a group of three or four together could be rigged up as a tent for the fishermen to sleep in.

The steamship that was to carry William had been built in England and shipped out in pieces to be rebuilt on the lake. It could sleep seventy-five passengers who were each asked, 'Do you want a hot or cold cabin?' – the hot cabins being near the engines. The meals were extras, but for those making a round trip on the lake the final bill was halved.

The ship departed shortly after dusk and reached Copacabana

at 2.00 a.m. It was a dull morning and at 6.00 a.m. the captain thought he would be sailing at 6.30 a.m. At 7.00 a.m. William told the chief pilot he would have liked to walk round the town, whereupon he volunteered to act as guide, saying if they were back in forty minutes all would be well. The only really interesting place was the old sanctuary church, the interior of which was very richly ornamented with gold and silver. The guide said it was a hundred years old and was built by the Conquistadors on their first arrival. They were late getting back to the ship because the guide walked slowly, being out of breath through talking and carrying too much beer, but still it was another half hour before the ship sailed.

The next port was Yungayo in Peru where the passengers stayed for the night. After a brief look at the fair in the plaza William went duck shooting which was said to be excellent. The first problem was that the ducks were too full of food to fly, even when clods of earth were thrown at them. When he rowed near them they swam far enough away to avoid capture or being run down. They did not fly at dusk or sunrise and William stuck to the rules of not hitting a sitting duck. He then walked round several small lakes in the area but it was the same story and the reeds were too thick to catch the birds by hand and throw them into the air.

Coya, the lake steamer

The frontier between Bolivia and Peru could be seen from a long way off. The Peruvians maintained an imposing customs house which was deserted because it was nearly 3 miles away from the nearest market. He crossed the border and walked for some miles along the lake on a fairly good track, several times satisfying his desire to see over the next rise and finally looking into Copacabana again. The scenery was attractive but here there was less cultivation and more cattle grazing. The Indian population was far higher than anywhere else in the Andes. Shortly after dark he was back on board the ship.

William woke long before daylight next morning intending to walk to Copacabana to rejoin the ship there on its return journey. Unfortunately the captain, without warning, left Yungayo an hour and a quarter early because he had a friend to see at the next port. One or two of the crew got left behind and had to race to the next port only to arrive a couple of minutes too late and the captain, with the possibility of making them lose all their pay, declined to wait even for a minute for them.

The only other port of call was Siripaca where a stack of 200 sacks of potatoes to be picked up could be seen a long way off. The ship's boats had to be lowered and sent in to collect the potatoes from the landing stage and transferred to the steamer which proved to be a very laborious process.

Later in the day they passed the Islands of the Sun and Moon where there was still a supply of Inca relics. The straits of Taquina leading in to the bay for Guaqui were narrow, and most remarkable was the telephone line which stretched from hilltop to hilltop across the channel with a considerable droop in the middle. There were many *balsas* on the lake fishing, some sailing quite fast.

Among the passengers landing at Copacabana was a very grand elderly lady waving her hands about in a stylish and benign manner. As she reached the shore her Indian servants rushed forward to do homage, bowing very low on her left side and kissing her hand. Each in turn was patted twice on the right shoulder, whereupon they stood up and started unloading her baggage.

On the return route the only passengers of interest were a party of nuns who went on a pilgrimage to Copacabana and enjoyed the views immensely, especially at Sorata, saying '*benito, lindo*'. William offered them his field glasses which were enjoyed by some, while others thought it was the work of the devil trying to improve on the eyes given by the Divine.

The ship reached Guaqui at 5.30 p.m. William stayed on board for the night but had to rush in the morning as the train was leaving the quay forty minutes early and was ready to go. At Tiahuanaco he thought he would purchase some souvenirs. He was overwhelmed by Indian children offering their wares and bought far more than he wanted, although he managed not to buy the expensive antique pottery which cost 1/6d (7½ new pence).

On return to La Paz William heard there was no chance of Smith recovering his properties in the near future so he took the train to Oruro, situated at the foot of some small hills where there were various tin and silver mines of little interest. The town was smaller and more compact than La Paz and the English people there more pleasant.

---

11 November 1925. Armistice Day was celebrated but not in the way one would wish. During the Silence the ex-servicemen sat with two cocktails in their hands and half an hour later more than half of them were drunk. The dinner in the evening had the customary interchange of telegrams to other towns. As usual it was a very cliquey meeting and all the officers had their special dinner in another building. After the dinner there was a dance which was attended by many non-service people. Each told a group of incredulous listeners of the stupendous efforts they made to get home in time for the War and how the British Government had pressed them to stay in Bolivia to maintain British prestige. As they all had senior jobs no scathing remarks were passed.

Soon after arriving in Oruro a man approached William in a rather blustering manner and demanded some tax. Disliking his face William disclaimed all knowledge of it and walked on. The

man, who was thoroughly dirty and had a grubby notebook did not look official, but he persisted until it became clear that he wanted road tax and if not it was prison. William had not heard of this tax and as the man had no official badge he took no notice and soon the man dropped behind, but shortly afterwards he came up again and demanded his tax of twelve shillings. William told him to do several amusing things with himself, and when he got really fed up told him to go to hell, and as an afterthought warned him that if he pestered him any more he would be run down to the local Superintendent of Police. The man seemed disappointed and William was proud of his effort to get rid of this shark.

Later in the day William mentioned this encounter to an acquaintance who confirmed the man was a genuine tax collector and by refusing to pay or show his identity card he was liable to various penalties, fines and imprisonment. William promptly went to the police station to be registered as an alien, and to pay his dues. By paying the tax in this manner the sum paid was halved, the street man being entitled to collect double. There was an alternative of doing two days work on the roads instead of paying tax but that was to be avoided by 'gringos'.

After church on Sundays it was the custom for the élite to be dressed in their finest clothes and to walk round the plaza to be admired. After a suitable length of time they drifted into a dance hall where they remained drinking and dancing until early afternoon – while William managed to get a game of tennis.

Oplaca

William met the general manager of the Patiño mine in Oruro who invited him to go and see the mine. He took the train across the Bolivian pampa of high desert to Machacamarca where he caught the connecting train on the mine's private line. He was accommodated at the Catavi mine hotel where precautions were taken to exclude undesirables. Barrande Hesse was working there

La Palca, Oplaca

and was anxious to get back to the comforts of his home in La Paz. He also promised to let William succeed him as head of the mine laboratory but the general manager disagreed and so William moved on again.

He intended to return to England and while passing through Uyuni again, he was offered a job at Oplaca, the third largest tin mine in Bolivia and one of the biggest tin producers in the world. William was offered a temporary job for the first couple of months after which it was expected that there would be plenty of scope for work in shaft-sinking and other work in which there would be considerable mining experience to be gained. At this time a new mill was being constructed and several hundred thousand pounds worth of machinery was lying dumped in hopeless confusion at Chocaya station. William's first job was to sort this out and have it sent up to the mine in the required order for the erection of the plant. A gantry had been erected but there was no tackle for it and there was no other appliance to handle the packing cases, some

of which weighed over ten tons. For some days everything had to be manhandled, some of the work being rather dangerous. With difficulty he obtained a 10-ton tackle, and sent men off to make a roadway up to the gantry.

For periods of bad weather there was plenty of work to do in the big corrugated-iron stores where there was no inventory and total confusion. Suitable accommodation was not available on site and William had to walk 3 miles each way from the hotel in Santa Ana at the main camp.

Christmas 1925. Tonkin gave the staff and their wives a dinner on Christmas night. A not very good quality champagne flowed and by the end of the meal a number of Bolivians were very drunk, enjoying themselves by shaking the bottles before opening them and spraying the foaming champagne round their heads, over the tables and ruining the ladies' dresses. Tonkin and the ladies left before the end of the meal.

New Year's Eve. The pay for this temporary work was not attractive and having tidied up the worst of the mess at the station William decided to take this opportunity to go to Valparaiso to collect the rest of his luggage from store so that it was available for when he went home in due course. He was sure the work he had started would proceed smoothly in his absence and on his return the better job should be ready for him to take.

On his way to Valparaiso he spent the first night at Uyuni again and after he had been in bed for some time he was awoken by a burst of musketry followed by shouting. At first his thoughts went back to the Communist uprising on the nitrate pampa, but then he discovered it was part of the New Year celebrations. Next a band appeared playing reed pipes which gave out a weird and wild sound as the musicians walked along the road. Indian dancers in national costume formed a long crocodile in pairs around the band and moved in a slow shuffling trot. Every now and then the men twirled the women across in front of them to the opposite side,

or the pair would twirl together going backwards or forwards to complete the circle to face the direction in which the crocodile was moving. Participants dropped out to consume a drink and then rejoined the dance. There was no singing although onlookers occasionally shouted advice or patriotic salutations and by 2.00 a.m. the streets were empty.

William took the train to Antofagasta where he was delayed for four days because all the boats were full. On the fifth day he managed to get a passage during which he sunbathed and got badly sunburned. One foot became very swollen and received further damage by a child jumping on it, the result being that for two or three days he had to stay in his room when he reached Valparaiso.

Since William's last visit there had been a lot of trouble in Gibbs & Co's store – one of his trunks had completely disappeared, two others were almost empty and the remaining boxes had been opened but few things removed. Luckily the thief had worked slowly and was caught before he had finished his work.

With the object of the trip completed, William spent the rest of the week at Quilpué where the Byrne family were staying and he enjoyed walking the children off their feet while they got their revenge in the swimming pool.

---

22 January 1926. On his way back to Oplaca William renewed some acquaintances in Antofagasta and reached Oplaca on 22 January 1926 without having any problems with the customs. The only thing he ever had to pay any duty on in Bolivia was his gun which had to be registered in La Paz where they stamped heavy numbers into the butt, despite his protestations.

He soon found that during his absence no work had been done on his new domain and he had to return to the main camp at Santa Ana. He now heard that Wayer, the Bolivian he had superseded, had already been superseded once before William's arrival. He was now in charge of transport and set out to make things difficult for William, by waylaying various working parties and transferring them to others in the company who were short of

labour. He removed William's heavy tackle for urgent work and it was obvious William would have to be on the spot if he was to compete with him. The weather was bad and so walking up and down, or travelling by any other means was difficult. He pressed hard for his work to be hurried forward and received many promises from the contractor as to the date he could go into the new building, but it never seemed to progress, and he still had no accommodation on site. The food at the Santa Ana Hotel was bad and by 10 February William, being fed up with all these delays, said he was moving the following night whether the house was ready or not. The office would be converted into a bedroom and the office would be moved into a small room at the back.

Thursday, 11 February 1926. William was packed and ready before 9.00 a.m. and phoned to enquire why his promised lorry was not there. It never came, while the floor of the room he intended using as an office had been dug up and was being deepened before reconstruction. No food or drink had arrived so another night was spent at Santa Ana.

Friday, 12 February 1926. Next day William informed the acting manager of the situation and said he would carry what he could on his back to the station and on arrival there would disconnect the phone and stop all work until his baggage arrived. This brought apologies and a lorry was summoned but never came. After an hour he was ready for combat but was told that a cart had been produced to take his things if he would wait to see it loaded up. After all this upset he proposed spending the next few Carnival days with Marrett, the engineer in charge at Siete Suyus.

The promised furniture had been handed over to someone else and for two more hours he was passed from Hoogland, the Dutch accountant, to others for help, the most likely person having just gone into hospital. Some of William's things were sent down but still no furniture and all the cooking utensils were missing, so he locked the office and said he had cut off the telephone. In the

evening he told Hoogland what he thought of him and Marrett said it was one of the best tickings off that he had heard from a junior to a senior.

Sunday, 14 February 1926. The Carnival started and by early morning many people were drunk. Early in the proceedings William met Wayer, who was largely responsible for so many things going wrong. They had an altercation and William failed to soothe him by suggesting that it would have been so much quicker if he had sent the lorries as promised. For a while he was tearful and then he threatened death and damnation. His idea of killing William made him laugh which only served to heighten Wayer's anger. William asked his host if there was any objection to their having a fight there and then to clear the air, but his request was refused. But Wayer could contain himself no longer and he picked up a chair with which to hit William and at that point others joined in and disarmed him. He glared at William as he continued to laugh and soon they each went to their respective houses.

By midday there was hardly a sober Bolivian in any of the camps and the lorry drivers were too drunk to replenish supplies, which was just as well as the road was very winding with a big drop into the creek on one side. All day columns of men and women trekked about the camp performing the Indian dance that William had seen at Uyuni. Each crocodile was headed by a leader bearing a banner on which he depended to keep his balance. A choir master was attached to most of the crocodiles and led the singing of songs in praise of the Carnival. Each line moved from open space to open space stopping in front of each 'gringo's' house and offering a large jar of chicha for their refreshment. The crowd remained until the jar was empty when they moved on to the next house. The band was never still and never sober, and when nominally stationary they swayed and shuffled their feet to the rhythm of the music.

The rooms in which the chicha was kept before being handed out stank appallingly. Whereas in Chile it was very young unfer-

mented wine, here it was a kind of local beer with *cingani* (a strong type of pisco) added to give it more kick. Often gin or any other alcoholic drink was also put in. To William's taste the drink was singularly unpalatable but it was very popular with the people to whom it was served.

Throughout the day there was a constant string of overseers and contractors going round to see each of the *gringo* heads of sections to have a few drinks with them to the greater glory of the Carnival and country. Each man endeavoured to outlast the others for by so doing he showed that he was in favour, and the rest were reluctant to leave as long as they could get free drinks without fear of having to return them. Fortunately for the staff this custom was recognized by the companies as being almost a necessity to retain labour and each member of staff was granted a drink allowance according to his rank. With Marrett there was seldom time to wash up the glasses and William soon became adept at swopping his full glass for an empty one on the table.

Just before William went to bed an American arrived in a panic. He was said to be one of the smartest mining engineers in Bolivia but he suffered from long drinking bouts when he would be drunk for the duration of up to four months, between which he would be teetotal; he was fearful of being offered a drink and expressed his dislike of seeing so many drunks. After two days he found the temptation so great he rode off into the mountains on a mule without warning and avoided human society until the holidays were over.

Each evening during the Carnival there was a dance at Santa Ana and at Siete Suyus. On the first night of the Carnival many people came up from the new mill to the Siete Suyus dance, returning to their own dance soon after midnight. This latter dance went on until dawn when the electrical engineer, returning to his bed somewhat the worse for drink, was rudely restored to sobriety when a brick hit him on the back of the head and others followed as he was chased home by an infuriated mob of Indians who wanted to kill him. He woke the other man sleeping in his house

and on seeing him the Indians cleared off, leaving the electrician much the worse for the encounter. It later transpired he was mistaken for the man in charge of the mill who, on hearing the Indians wanted him, drove all the way back to Santa Ana without lights and locked himself in his house. When his wife returned at the end of the dance he refused to let her in so she went for assistance and when the party threatened to break in the door he finally opened it.

Tuesday, 16 February 1926. During the day Marrett and New were invested with diadems of silver filigree roses. It was the annual custom that if the men in charge were popular and had been there for a year the workmen clubbed together to make a presentation to the heads of sections. All the Europeans gathered together and were draped in streamers, women taking pride in adding to the quantity. This time they were presented with suitably inscribed diadems of silver filigree roses costing about £20 each. After the presentations the foremen and their wives produced champagne and afterwards followed the recipients to their respective houses to be offered beer, gin or vermouth.

Wednesday, 17 February 1926. The general manager was expected back at the camp but the lorry drivers were still too drunk to drive. At 11.00 a.m. William was about to walk down to meet the train when the dancers appeared again. He postponed his departure until after lunch as he had some parcels to carry and thought it best to wait until they had gone. Next the '*maestranza*' came up, another lot of dancers who had previously involved William. They decided that William and a colleague, New, had not been to a Carnival before and did not enjoy it in the spirit they most appreciated. For William and New to see it at its best they first stopped at Marrett's house until there was no drink left. With added energy they took the two men further afield. At first William was at the end of the column but this was not thought to be in accordance with his dignity and he was placed behind the man carrying the

banner. New desperately wanted to go home, and so did William, but they could not. They climbed up the mountain to the bakery and charged straight in without losing speed, passing from bright sunshine into darkness, William leading his lady of the moment still at the head of the column. They were greeted with showers of flour coming from everywhere, and being the first in William got the full blast of it, which binded him for a moment and he had to be taken outside to clear his eyes. Others came out to explain it was the usual custom of the place and they thought William knew about it. He had to pretend he enjoyed it and then followed round after round of drinks and a series of *cueca* danced in a stuffy overcrowded barn. A few went outside onto a narrow bridge with no rails to continue dancing where a loose stone nearly caused William to fall to the rocks below. Pisco, chicha, gin and beer were circulated and after a round of each had been drunk the dance circuit resumed, and still some remained sober. William explained that being new to the height he could not drink as much as the locals, but they did not know how many glasses slipped unseen to the ground in the darkness inside the barn. He did not escape until 5.00 p.m. when, filthy dirty and still covered in flour, he went back on foot and met Tonkin, the general manager.

Tonkin heard all about the fracas and realized it was mostly related to the Carnival. Wayer complained about William cutting off the telephone and learnt for the first time that the telephone line had been down for days and there was no chance of repairing it.

After the Carnival frolics there was a national shortage of flour and bread and it was a week before any bread could be bought from the train.

Eggs lasted a long time but it was difficult to tell whether they were bad because the water test did not work, sometimes bad eggs sank and sometimes good eggs floated. William's main diet was porridge and ham. The prices in the grocery store (run by the company) were very high, except for tonic water because someone had ordered some cases of it but had left before it arrived. It was

sold for 1/6d a bottle and no-one wanted it at that price, so it was then given away as prizes at bridge parties, but it was still left behind. It was now down to a penny a bottle so William bought a case and finding it to be in excellent condition he bought three more cases. There was suddenly a run on the remaining supplies lead by Tonkin, Marrett and Hoogland until it was finished.

---

21 February 1926. There was still no sign of the furniture and William heard from Smith that things at Fabulosa had improved, so he offered his resignation in very firm tones. He was given a week to reconsider and the next day his furniture arrived from La Paz.

Early March 1926. Further heavy machinery arrived and William was expected to handle 8- and 9-ton items with 3-ton tackle as Tonkin did not know the heavy tackle was removed contrary to his orders. This tackle was now recovered.

The following night the international train arrived having had some delays and as a result they had insufficient fuel to get to the next station. William started the refuelling job at 9.00 p.m., long after dark, with no lamps available; 400-lb drums had to be lifted onto the top of the engine and tipped up. Lifting the drums up singly in the 10-ton differential tackle was slow and safe and it took a long time to build up a framework on empty drums with timber under 20 foot long to reach the top of the engine, and then roll the full drums up. After five hours the engine driver decided he had sufficient oil to get him to Uyuni.

---

14 March 1926. This was when the tennis match between Oplaca and Aramayo, Franke & Co. took place. The other team had many more staff to select from, played every day and their team included the Bolivian second-best player. The Oplaca team were all poor players, they only played on Sundays and William could beat any one of them in singles 6-0. At that altitude singles was hard work being rather breathless, the ball had a much straighter flight than usual and bounced very high on the hard court.

The match started at noon and, as expected, Oplaca lost every set, 6-2, 6-5, 6-0, by which time they were glad to have lunch. After lunch they accepted a singles challenge between the best players and William had to play the Bolivian who had beaten their number one player fairly decisively the previous weekend. In less than five minutes William had lost four games using his old fishing net racquet with slack strings. He then picked up the nearest good-looking racquet (which belonged to the visiting team's general manager) and took the next four games easily, to the delight of the crowd. His opponent claimed many points in his desperation in spite of protests from the spectators, however, William lost the set by drinking two bottles of beer when changing ends. The crowd wanted to put money on a return game but it was declined. Other members of the Oplaca team were then severely beaten and finally Locke and William took on their best pair again who had beaten them 6-0 in the morning. It was a great game and the spectators became very excited. The players were exhausted but Oplaca was triumphant as William and Locke won 12-10, and in the last ten games they averaged over three deuces per game.

---

21 March 1926. This was William's last day. He hurriedly settled up and said his farewells at Santa Ana. Tonkin took him to the station and still gave him the chance to change his mind, but Smith had got a position ready for him to go to. They reached the station as the train arrived but William had not finished packing; fortunately he had made friends with the station master who kept the engine busy shunting trucks about for over an hour. The train was ready to go as soon as William's baggage was put on board and he had a great send-off from the European colony.

CHAPTER VIII

Fabulosa

25 March 1926

illiam arrived back at La Paz where he had two days to spare before Smith was ready to go out to the mine, during which time he heard more about Smith's problems. A minority of the old shareholders were dissatisfied with their pickings and they enlisted the sympathy of the President of the Republic who sent troops and police to hold the property until their claims were met. Smith enlisted the help of the Vice-President and the head of the police. A party of police were sent out to take over the property and make it safe for Smith to return, but they were driven off. Much money went in litigation and bribery before the property was recovered. There was still some opposition and some arrests were made, including one of the senior policeman from the other side. Maxwell Williams left to take over Milluni officially only two days earlier and for a week he was in imminent danger of losing his life.

27 March 1926. William accompanied Smith on the car ride to La Union going first to Milluni. They took a local expert with them to quote probable costs of various schemes for increased water power.

The road out of La Paz was excellent but the long climb to the plateau involved stopping several times to wait for the engine to cool. The road was now a track from which the bigger stones had been removed so they could travel fairly fast until they reached the water reservoir and aerodrome, after which they had to slow down on account of many boulders. At about the halfway point there

was a steep descent on a greasy track on the edge of a hill, and being inadequately banked up it sloped almost at right angles to the intended direction. For the rest of the journey they travelled at right angles to the slope of every hill, bumping and skidding in a fearsome manner. It was essential to hold tight on to the roof of the car to prevent being brained every few moments and Smith was anxious to get out and walk every time things got worse. After two hours Milluni could be seen at the far end of the valley. Half a mile short of the camp there was a field gun perched on a small knoll covering the road, and beside it there was a fire trench and a loop-holed shelter. The gun turned out to be a well-built dummy, but the trenches had been used earlier against the police sent out by Smith's party.

The camp was prepared for defence because their predecessors were under the impression that Smith intended storming it and so defences were constructed. Trenches were dug near the buildings, and the offices and staff houses had had all convenient windows

There was a dummy field gun perched on a small knoll covering the road

sandbagged. Where the defences were inconvenient they were left unprotected. The gunmen inside had been drinking a lot during which they had filled the walls of the living room with bullet holes. They also left behind them a number of booby traps such as sticks of dynamite in the coal, so Maxwell Williams, the man in charge of Milluni, found it necessary to send one of the old foremen in to the mine levels first, to aid the man's memory as to where the traps had been laid.

The camp is situated at the foot of Huayna Potosi, 23,500 feet high, one of the highest mountains in South America, which was said to have never been climbed, the top part being the most difficult to reach. The top 3,000 feet are always covered with snow and many long glaciers could be seen dipping into gorges. William renamed the mountain 'Windy Potosi' because it was the coldest and most windy camp in South America.

That night William had a cold bath, there being no hot water, but he did not repeat it. The bedding was scanty and the blankets had shrunk to such an extent they were virtually useless as he seemed to stick out in all directions.

Sunday, 28 March 1926. In the morning Smith and William walked round the water supplies formulating schemes to take up the waste water. By afternoon they were drenched by heavy showers and Smith, already in a very bad mood then found he had lost one of his fur gloves in the snow. They searched in every unlikely direction in the snow and slush. Finally by retracing the mule tracks in the snow the glove was found where Smith had dismounted in the morning.

Monday, 29 March 1926. Smith and William were to ride to La Union which was to be William's headquarters. Smith was in a bad mood having had a poor night and was now suffering from a stiff back. William was given the best mule but it too was in a bad mood, flicking its ears and rolling its eyes. The helpers shied away from it but an Indian held it reluctantly, while it continued

to play up a bit as William mounted because he did not like the heavy haversack. Once mounted the mule behaved well except for occasionally trying to roll. They were followed by quite a train of carriers and wasted much time waiting for them because, although they did not know it, they were carrying a lot of cash. The track lay up a long gorge leading to a pass 16,000 feet high.

It took six hours to reach La Union which was larger and better than Milluni in every way. The camp was further from the mountains and felt warmer despite being about 14,500 feet above sea level. There was no sign of war but the sanitary conditions were bad. The staff rooms were in good condition but the mill and other gear were all in a dilapidated state.

Tuesday, 30 March 1926. After a survey of the water power schemes Smith, Haynes and William planned to see the San Alberto mine, one of a group of mines the company was supposed to have taken over, but which had somehow remained in the hands of the vendors. The mules were out in the morning and William observed they were very small – if he mounted one his feet would be on the ground; he also saw the saddles slip off their backs several times, so although his colleagues elected to ride William thought it safer and quicker to walk. It was a short but stiff climb and William arrived soon after the riders, finding them struggling with their lamps which either emitted a small flame with vast quantities of smoke but no light, or they half exploded, or refused to give any sign of light.

They finally entered a vast cavern and scrambled and crawled into many nooks and crannies taking samples containing tin everywhere. It seemed to be one of the biggest finds in that wonderful country of mining freaks. There was a suppressed atmosphere of pleasure as they reflected the boundary had recently been moved to more suitable places, thereby invalidating old claims, and the present owner had no idea of how rich the mine was having never been inside it or had a professional report made on it.

Wednesday, 31 March 1926. William started work in the laboratory

The main area of ore in San Alberto mine

which he found to be the most dirty, untidy, disorganized and ill-fitted that he had ever seen. There was no apparatus or chemicals for even a simple tin assay, although such work was supposed to have been carried out even within the last few days. Bottles were incorrectly labelled and many essential articles were absent. It took two days to clear out the junk, sort out what was left and send a refitting list to La Paz. The store then had to be thoroughly cleaned.

At the weekend William and Haynes went to the lake to shoot. Haynes with his small rifle was to drive the birds towards William who hid in the valley at the opposite end of the lake with his rifle. For half an hour William lay on his tummy in a pool of cold water and nothing happened. Getting cold and tired of this William decided to join Haynes and do some shooting. He shot a goose in the middle of the lake which was out of reach and drifting towards the far end. While walking round William fell into two hidden pools which were cold and slimy. The goose was by now near the edge but the deep and greasy mud still kept the bird out of reach. Later in the afternoon William saw and smelled an Indian cooking his bird.

By the middle of April the company's buyer in La Paz decided

most of William's indent was unobtainable so he went to make the purchases himself as Smith was dancing with rage at the delay in getting assays done and samples were mounting fast. The purchases were handed in to the office to be sent up by the next lorry. Bromine was hard to obtain so William carried a bottle of it with an ill-fitting stopper back to the hotel. The smell in his room was such that the bottle had to be put out on the balcony where it forced the man in the next room to close his window.

Next morning William intended leaving the hotel at 8.30 a.m. but no-one was up. After ringing the bell for some time he obtained a cup of coffee but no bill, so he rang the bell for a further hour and was told the bill was 'just coming'. Finally the bell was disconnected by the waiter. Meanwhile the chauffeur, who had arrived at 8.00 a.m. was getting cold and annoyed. Getting no further replies to the bell William disconnected it his end and left, leaving no forwarding address.

Before leaving La Paz the chauffeur confirmed he had seen the boxes loaded onto the lorry going to the mine although on arrival the lorry was there but no boxes. Smith knew the man in the office and realizing he was mainly to blame sent a note for the goods to be forwarded immediately. After another week the goods had still not arrived and more notes were sent after which Smith went out himself to find out the cause of the delay. On the way he passed the lorry carrying the goods, but that did not save the man in the office from being sacked for negligence. He was not interested in these boxes because he never bought anything unless there was a good discount for himself.

The backlog of work was enormous and William worked eighty hours in the first week and the second one too. For the first day he had an assistant who deserted after that.

In the high altitudes of the Andes the Bolivian and Peruvian Indians had a habit of chewing coca. This substance helped them resist fatigue, hunger and cold and in moderation was thought to be good for them. However they usually took an excess of it which damaged their teeth and shortened their lives considerably. In earlier

times there had been efforts to suppress its use but even the death penalty did not act as a deterrent. Usually they had a wad pressed into one cheek and a handful of leaves would last two days. Today tourists going to hotels at high altitudes are given a drink of coca tea on arrival to help avoid altitude sickness.

At the end of April, while assisting with the weekly pay, William had a swollen cheek and was accused of chewing coca. Next morning he was in bed with a severe toothache to which he administered a mustard plaster which took all the skin off his cheek and failed to relieve the pain. On Tuesday he went to La Paz where Casey, the secretary, said Herrera (Herrero means blacksmith) was the best dentist in town. He picked up all kinds of pincers and alarming tools and worked in cold blood saying it was dangerous to use any anaesthetic at that altitude. William soon learned the meaning of the word pain. The first effort only drew blood, while the second produced several howls before pushing Herrera away and demanding a break. He rested in the waiting room for ten minutes while he treated a young lady in a similar manner, after which she was carried out of the room semi-conscious. At the third attempt he managed to break off the tooth next to the one he was supposed to be extracting by levering on it. In so doing he cut William's tongue and had torn many holes in his gums but failed to extract the tooth. At this point William pushed him off and wished he had pushed much harder. After being told that the job would have been easy had William given him a chance, William left aching too much to attempt answering in Spanish.

He felt like having a few words with Casey but he kept out of the way. Another man took him to see a second dentist with whom William proposed making an appointment. He wanted to see the nature of the job and before he knew what was happening, the dentist had his grip on the tooth and with one more howl the tooth came out relatively painlessly. The dentist then asked if William had been to a butcher or slaughterhouse before seeing him and on hearing the name 'Herrera', let out a howl of joy.

William went to bed to recover but Maxwell Williams found

him and stayed from 3.00 to 6.30 p.m. William sent Maxwell to get a bottle of brandy which he (Maxwell) enjoyed immensely and generously allowed William a couple of tots. His crowning annoyance was to invite William to dine with a couple of English ladies in spite of the state of his face and temper.

Comment

William found it necessary to take responsibility for ordinary forms of decency at La Union. Although Smith expected his staff to shave before breakfast he turned up twice running without having shaved himself. As he left the dining room on the second occasion William handed him a shaving brush with an apology for not sending it round earlier. Smith was shocked at the time but an American businessman arrived unexpectedly for lunch and Smith was glad he looked respectable and related the story to the visitor. Attention was drawn to the clean table cloth which was not special for his benefit and a remark that everyone washed their hands before meals drew scowls from the two who seldom did, while William concealed his hands as they were covered in chemical stains. Despite the apparent disrespect William was the only person who was allowed in Smith's room after work, a privilege he treated with due care.

Some of the staff were hardly accustomed to living in a house and would scarcely have been considered clean even if they lived outdoors. They did not know how to use a toilet and usually stood on the seat, so William built a special place for them away from the house. Those used to normal toilet procedures were each supplied with a special seat which they carried about with them with as dignified an air as the situation admitted.

In May and June William was working thirteen to fifteen and a half hours daily until he was up to date. His only escapes were the occasional trip to the mill in connection with production sampling or trips to other mines in the La Union group whenever there was a report that gunmen had appeared to claim the mine. These trips seemed almost suicidal as Haynes and William were

faced with up to a dozen armed men who had the advantage of being underground in the dark while they had to chase them out from the light. They did not have a high opinion of their opponents and on one occasion they arrived at the Esperanza (meaning hope) mine to chase away eight desperate men at which vital moment Haynes found he had forgotten his gun. Once again the gunmen cleared off on seeing William and Haynes approach.

Soon they were given a chief of police to assist and legalize these expeditions. He was told to make some arrests but the men cleared out too quickly, having stopped work for only an hour or so.

William was longing for a long walk again and now had a chance to climb to the San Alberto glacier. It was much longer and higher than expected and he only reached the top at sunset. The moon was bright so he returned at a leisurely pace and was surprised to meet a search party of three a few hundred yards from camp. Smith was there and, to the amusement of all, fell into the river below the house giving a fine demonstration of swearing. They arrived back at camp at 9.00 p.m. A week later William repeated the walk and again a search party was considered but they decided to wait

San Alberto glacier

until 10.00 p.m. He eventually persuaded them it was safer for him not to have to hurry and to trust he would get back safely.

Having done a few five-hour walks he now proposed an eight- or nine-hour trek over the San Alberto glacier and down the far side into the Songa trail and circle back to camp. To be clear of work he stayed in the laboratory until 3.00 a.m. on Sunday and by 10.30 a.m. he set off with two Airedale Terriers that were on loan to the camp. On reaching the top of the glacier he was tired but thoughts of turning back were soon dismissed for the long screes ahead were calling and the dogs were revelling in the snow. It was fun racing the dogs down the loose detritus (rock gravel) before reaching another glacier which had to be crossed more carefully. A long descent of about 7,000 feet followed when, nearing the bottom, they met a dead end, by which time William was feeling very tired. There was a small bluff down which William could climb but the dogs would not attempt it, so they had to climb up about 4,000 feet before finding another way down.

William passed several veins of tin and one of silver ore and pocketed samples of each. On reaching the bottom again the dogs decided it was equally impassable. It was now late and William was exhausted. He clambered down a few feet and coaxed one dog into his grasp, heaved her off the rocks and leaned down to drop her to the ground below, but before he had completed the exercise the other dog jumped onto him and the three rolled down a steep slope. William was wet and a bit shocked, but none of them was hurt. They hurried down to a height at which straggling grass grew and crossed the bottom several times looking for the Songa trail. Each time he had to cross a stream, about 10 yards wide and 3 feet deep, which runs into the Amazon. In the dark it seemed like a mighty river with huge boulders at the bottom. By now William kept falling, either over the boulders or in the long grass and it was taking increasingly longer to get up after each fall, so that eventually he was having to take a short rest before moving on again.

After another two hours he came to an impassable cliff but by

walking along the foot of it he accidentally found a narrow winding path – the track he had been looking for. It was about three quarters of a mile long and very steep and took another two hours to negotiate for William had had nothing to eat all day and by now he was so exhausted he had to rest after every few steps.

He was desperately hungry and started sipping the snow water which was refreshing and he drank ever increasing amounts of it with no ill effects. After the steep climb the slope was moderate again but he was now at a height where the air and wind from the snow were bitterly cold and where it was not unusual for two inches of ice to form during the night. It was too cold to sit down and rest and William estimated he would not get back before 4.00 a.m. After midnight the moonlight made it easier to walk and climb so the last pass was accomplished rather faster then expected. The descent on the other side was quick and the final walk back along a good track should have taken ninety minutes but in the event took longer. On arrival back at camp the two dogs slunk into their kennels exhausted but bucked up when William brought them what had been left for his dinner which, when hot might have been excellent, but cold it was greasy and unpalatable. William managed to find something cold to eat and Smith appeared with a stiff whisky as daylight was beginning to appear. William went to bed where he stayed until lunchtime, when the young maintained he had been on the tiles in La Paz all night.

A glutton for punishment, William decided to do the same walk in reverse the following Sunday as Smith wanted to see the veins of tin William had found, but via an easier route. He started back along the Songa trail and at its highest point the Indians had made their offering to the gods of a single stone carried up from the bottom, or some farm product or other gift. These gifts were essential lest the gods rolled a stone on them, or created a fog to get them completely lost. They included cigarettes, matches, oranges, lemons, guavas or bits of rags and once donated they were never touched by anyone else. In daylight the descent was easy and this time William carried food for himself and the one dog

accompanying him. The track up the valley had an easier gradient and by the time it was getting late William realized he was walking in the wrong direction. While there was still enough light he found shelter from the wind behind some rocks and there he had supper and prepared to sleep for the night. The dog took the best position and after being turned out of it made himself very comfortable under William's legs. This was not so good for William as the dog wore a spiked collar round his neck which was firmly closed by a padlock, and every time the dog moved the spikes drove into William's legs. The stars were bright and the air crisp. At about 5 a.m. there was a little moonlight and William and dog started climbing again. He thought he was near Milluni and considered having breakfast there with Griffiths who had taken over from Maxwell Williams. Approaching the top of the valley the climb got worse and near the top the dog jibbed. The barrier to get to Milluni and breakfast was too great, and the more tantalizing hearing the dogs at the camp barking.

By 10 a.m. William reached the place where he should have turned off the main valley. It was hard to recognize due to a steep convex slope with no track up it, and little hope of bringing Smith and a camping party to prospect in luxury. After climbing some distance grass fires were started below and the wind carried them up the slope towards William. He hurried on and then found more fires above him but at the top of the vegetation level there were many bare spots to give shelter if necessary although the smoke was dense and William did not wish to spend a second night out.

At one point it was difficult to judge where to pass through the blazing fires and often the dog had to be carried because the ground was too hot. On the flat land below the bottom glacier a mist blew up and it was difficult to keep the right direction. Having passed the glacier the scree became exceedingly difficult, each step forward bringing debris from above, and sometimes after climbing some distance a slide brought William and dog back to the starting point. After several attempts he found a fairly easy route through the

rocks but near the top the dog gave up and another half an hour was lost.

By sundown the mist was settling fast and the night looked black and cold. He was too high to sleep out in safety and in the fading light hastened towards the edge of the glacier. For the last few hundred yards it was dark, bitterly cold and he was frequently moving over or clutching the ice. At the bottom, as soon as he was clear of the moraine, he could move faster and became annoyed when he saw rockets going up in several places thinking it was a search party looking for him. He fired his pistol a few times to let them know his whereabouts and pushed on. Back at the camp he found the search party had not thought of moving out again being convinced he had dug a hole in the snow at the greatest possible height.

During the walk William only saw six squirrels, two viscachas (a nocturnal rodent like a chinchilla, about 22 inches long, living in a burrow) and two foxes which were near Indian huts on the Songa trail.

On another weekend William's walk had to be cancelled as he was called upon to assist in entertaining Stodart's friends. He dressed to perfection with shining boots and spotless cream riding breeches – attire that had probably never been seen in such perfection in a South American mining camp before. Smith was in a foul mood when William called on him, but this apparition changed his mood instantly and he was introduced to the guests as 'our mannequin'. The men of the party were not at their best having been up most of the previous night and two of them retired to sleep for the entire evening. They had attended a surprise party at the Legation and Gudgeon, duly warned, had appeared in a nightshirt over his evening clothes, with night cap and night light asking who dared disturb the sleep of His Majesty's representative.

June 1926. At the end of June these walks were interrupted by a return to the laboratory. From 22 to 29 June it was undergoing alterations, repairs and repainting. William resumed his assaying

work on 30 June and the following afternoon Haynes entered excitedly having found a new and valuable load of tin. He hastily completed the necessary papers and asked William to take them by hand to Smith in La Paz to enable him to apply for the mining claim. Smith was occupied attending a number of dinners in honour of Stodard's impending return to England. William had to take the document personally as the sending of a document of this nature to La Paz could be a source of profit to many people, either by selling the plans to a third party and delaying delivery for a few hours, or by the bearer telling the company that he had completed the negotiations for selling unless a better price was offered by the company. The lorry driver would delight in such an opportunity and there was at least one senior member of staff who was known to have profited handsomely in this way.

4 July 1926. On return William resumed work in the laboratory and after dinner on 4 July he was told he had to make a rush visit to Fabulosa because Maxwell Williams was reported to be seriously ill. After seeing the doctor he had resigned from the company, apparently in a disturbed mental state. William was to escort Maxwell Williams back to La Paz while a German took over his position.

William finished his work in the laboratory by midnight and went to bed. He was up again the following morning before daylight and Losey was to accompany him on the long ride. It was very cold outside and it took time to locate the cook and persuade him to get out of bed to prepare breakfast. Despite the delay they were on their way at 6.00 a.m. when there was a glimmer of light in the sky. They started walking for the first two minutes and could see well enough to trot slowly down the road. They continued at a steady pace for the next hour at which point they left the road and continued the steady trot for the next two hours as they crossed the rolling downs of the pampa region, much of which was swamp. Occasionally it was necessary to dismount and lead the mules because of the ice on the ground. Small rivers had iced up and

were particularly treacherous requiring careful negotiation to avoid injury to man or beast. The high peak of the Huayna Potosi dominated the whole countryside.

The first half of the route was the easiest and taken at a fast pace for that altitude. They reached the halt at 11.00 a.m. where they fed and watered the mules and had an hour's rest. Only very poor quality straw was available for the mules but somehow the animals in South America manage to survive such conditions.

After the break they rode along the south side of a lake 4 miles long. The air was sweet and clear and the scenery was pretty rather than grand. At the end of the lake there was an abrupt climb of several hundred feet where after every few paces William and the mules had to stop and recapture their breath. Looking back from the top Lake Titicaca could be clearly seen and from this distance (about 25 miles or more) looked no bigger than a pond.

They came to a second and third lake, each with a bigger climb at the far end, and it was after the third lake they reached the highest point, said to be well over 20,000 feet high. Curiously walking here was not as strenuous as walking at 20,000 feet on Huayna Potosi. It was a formidable place to be amidst the big glaciers, more appearing below than above.

Time was of the essence so to hasten the descent they dismounted and drove the mules ahead. It was at least 12 miles long, varying from being steep to very steep and covering a drop of about 9,000 feet. The scenery was grand, very bleak and inhospitable, with no birds even on the lakes. After the halt they only saw two Indians, a few llamas and vicuña and many skeletons of mules and llamas that had died on the trail.

It was getting dark before they reached the bottom of the valley and there remained a huge climb ahead where they were rewarded by magnificent views. A good track wound round the side of the hill on a steep gradient, and as they climbed they crossed a long spur running far out into a wide valley which opened into the Beni country. Thousands of feet below dense cloud masses stretched out far towards the borders of Brazil, looking like a great white

sea, while here and there were some great pinnacles of rock standing high above the clouds.

It was 7.00 p.m. when they reached their destination at last, tired, hungry and very thirsty. The camp was dreadful and very distressing. The accommodation was awful and only extreme hunger enabled them to eat the food. It was now easy to see why Maxwell Williams had resigned. Although La Union and Milluni received ample good food from La Paz, none reached Williams at his isolated camp. A little was sent out but was looted on the way and for a time Williams and his companion had to survive on native food alone. After being in charge at Milluni, a camp of plenty, he had now lost all his energy and could not do the work.

William brought out a bottle of whisky in a siphon bottle (the first Williams had seen since arriving here) but there was no spare bottle to put it in, so they tried to aerate the whisky and then squirt it into plain water in the hope that the long column of bubbles that came out would mix to make a whisky and soda. The experiment was not a success, but the whisky did help make the night pass pleasantly. William maintained his capacity for spinning yarns all night without becoming boring, but was no longer the same man he had been.

Tuesday, 6 July. Next morning William walked round the underground workings and found zinc, lead, tin, silver and other minerals mixed in a jumble; every few paces there were pockets of various minerals which should have reduced exploration costs. A pocket of molybdenite had been thrown out leaving a most beautiful cave with walls that appeared to be covered in black velvet which in the dim light seemed like fairy land.

In the afternoon William and Maxwell Williams climbed the 2,000 feet to the top of the mountain and spent some hours among the glaciers gazing upon the veins of tin.

They decided a day was adequate to familiarize the German who was taking over as he had been on the property before and planned leaving at 8.00 a.m. next morning. To ensure a prompt departure

they told themselves 7.00 a.m. and told the mule man 6.00 a.m. (but he did not believe what he was hearing).

Wednesday, 7 July. By morning the men in the camp were already showing open disrespect to the German who was now in charge.

The mules arrived very late because it took a long time to find them. Within a few moments the best mule bolted off into the distance taking with him Maxwell Williams's private saddle and bridle and William's (Chads) head rope. After that the baggage mules cleared off with the luggage and it took an hour to catch them again. William's baggage disappeared but reappeared in a mysterious way, and the man sent to collect rope for fixing the baggage delivered it and then disappeared never to be seen again.

After a frustrating morning they finally departed at 10.00 a.m. and William agreed to take the invalid's preferred route via Milluni. On leaving the camp the track went down an almost precipitous side of the mountain for 2,000 feet. Crossing the valley they climbed an easier gradient to a greater height, and in the following few hours crossed several more valleys diagonally, finally arriving at lower levels. They had to dismount several times because the steep slopes could only be negotiated by leading the mules, one particular slope appearing to be impossible to descend even on foot.

At one point Williams strayed from the ill-defined goat track and ended up wading up to his knees in a thick muddy bog. Sometimes the track disappeared altogether, at other times it bifurcated, and where there was an alternative track it seemed they always took the wrong one.

They had to cross a couple of screes on foot and on the larger one the invalid's mule received a cut which bled copiously. To add to his difficulties he somehow got a nail in his boot and was too lame to walk, so he rode William's mule and led his own from 1.00 p.m. while William walked behind and encouraged the mule to go on when necessary.

By 3.00 p.m. they were hungry and on opening the lunch packet

found the sandwiches of bread and meat were inedible; the tin of fruit looked appetizing but they had no means of opening it. They considered trying to shoot the top off with a pistol but by a strange piece of luck a travelling padre came along from the Beni country and they traded the tin for some excellent coffee, bananas, guavas and tangerines.

After a final long descent they reached the familiar Songa trail at 4.00 p.m. The invalid was very tired and William proposed spending the night near these houses where it would not be too cold during the night. The moon was in its last quarter and there was little chance of getting in until midnight. The rest of the trail was said to be well defined but neither of them was familiar with it. Despite his tiredness the invalid insisted on getting to Milluni that night, no matter how late it was. His mule was now going quite soundly but despite having had half an hour's rest he made slow progress and was often half a mile behind William.

At 6.00 p.m., shortly after dusk, they reached the foot of the last big climb where the trail zigzagged up the mountain side and it was very difficult to follow in the dark. The bottom half was in deep shadow from overhanging cliffs and progress was again very slow having to be taken step by step. The mules were nervous and tried alternately to jump or to hang back and snort. Twice William went off the path and only the reins saved him from a very long and painful slide down. Each time they scrambled back to the snorting mule they took even greater care.

At the top half of the climb the gradient was severe but they were able to proceed at a more normal pace, and by 9.00 p.m. they finally saw the lights of Milluni, although it was not until 10.30 p.m. that they actually arrived there.

William thought the ride was about 40 miles, saving about 15 miles on the other route, but this was infinitely worse and in many places they could easily have missed the trail completely.

In Milluni there was no watchman, the staff houses were deserted, the mill was barely working – all the senior men being absent from their shift – and the mill house was filled with clouds of steam.

All those on duty were sitting about or sleeping and no-one was doing any work. On recognizing Williams there was a sudden burst of activity, but none of the headmen appeared, being too drunk to be able to stand. Griffiths, the man in charge, had been called to La Paz for the night and the camp had taken this opportunity for a binge.

It took two hours to get the mules watered, fed and settled for the night and to get the cook up to prepare a meal for them. Smith could not be contacted on the telephone that night and work resumed as normal the following morning with many requests that nothing should be said about what had been seen the night before.

July 1926. Haynes and William went to investigate some old Spanish workings and after opening the entrance they allowed a couple of days for ventilation and to let out the gasses. The Spanish had driven through thick rock to a height of 5 to 7 feet and then came a shaft 3 feet high through wet clay. It was perfectly made and they came out with their faces covered in red clay having seen few signs of tin or silver.

Smith had long promised William a visit to the Fabulosa group of company's properties and with yet another postponement William decided to go it alone. There was no mule suitable for the distance so he went off on foot the following weekend. The route covered 20 miles along the Songa trail and then across a series of valleys leading down into the Beni country. Kit was reduced to a minimum with camera and essentials in a rucksack, making a total load of 30 pounds.

William set off at 5.30 a.m. and when crossing the stream within the first minute, he slipped on ice and his shoes were filled with lumps of ice and cold water. These shoes had been saturated in castor oil to make them waterproof and William had to wear them as his other boots and shoes were worn out and would not have stood the journey. Within the first 2 miles his feet warmed up the water in the shoes and they gradually dried up. He walked along the now familiar deep valley leading to the stiff climb up the Songa

trail. The sun appeared at 8.30 a.m. and as he descended the scenery became less imposing, the snow-capped peaks giving place to grass-covered convex slopes. The number of places where there had been recent landslides decreased as he reached the bottom of the valley where the grass was long and rank.

It was now getting very hot and by noon, having walked for over 20 miles, he saw the first cluster of houses outside La Paz, and two trees. He asked one of the inhabitants for directions and went northwards up another valley, stopping for lunch an hour later. He refreshed himself by washing his feet in cold, clear water and enjoyed an hour's rest in the long grass. From then on he climbed for hours, the track slowly bending round until he found himself going directly towards La Union again. He had followed the main track and valley but somehow had failed to reach the proposed destination.

Darkness was approaching and there seemed no point in climbing to colder parts, so William settled down to camp early in some long grass well sheltered from the wind. After a short rest William heard sounds of blasting. The position of the Fabulosa camp had never been ascertained on paper and the distance across the mountains was unknown. Before starting the general direction was pointed out and it was 'somewhere beyond that mountain'.

William was now 'beyond that mountain' and on hearing these blasts he got up and went ahead thinking he would soon see lights. After climbing several thousand feet he heard more blasting but soon realized that it was ice cracking and falling on the ice fields that now surrounded him. He was extremely lucky to find an old disused Indian hut where he made himself as warm and comfortable as possible. He was well supplied with extra underclothing and there was plenty of clean straw in the thatching and good solid walls, but this was not enough to keep out the bitter cold. He shivered all night and each time he awoke from the cold he pulled down a bit more straw from the roof.

William stayed in his shelter until the sun was warm and then went out to a sunny spot on the rocks to thaw out. He thought he

was about 7 miles north of La Union and headed off in that direction. After an hour's climb he stopped for breakfast which consisted of sandwiches washed down by the whisky he was supposedly taking out to Maxwell Williams. After a little more basking in the sun he started on the final steep portion at 9.00 a.m. This took four hours of hard going, suffering the usual problems of slipping backwards on the screes. On reaching the top he saw below on the other side a long and nasty glacier and from this viewpoint it was impossible to get to either edge to creep down comfortably. The descent was undignified as he sat on the snow most of the time, cautiously drumming his heels into the ground to be watchful of crevasses, from each of which he scrambled back hastily. The glacier and moraine (debris from a glacier) below took another four hours to cross, reaching camp two hours later, shortly after sunset.

By now no-one in the camp expressed any surprise at William's 'accommodation' and they knew that he might or might not reach his destination, but in any event would return there having camped out somewhere for at least one night.

William needed to see Smith who was in La Paz and so he drove there in an open lorry, arriving in La Paz after dark. It was a bitterly cold journey and the driver went at an alarming rate. He saw Smith and expressed his concerns about Maxwell Williams's health. William returned to La Union with the general manager on 11 July but it was Williams who was now too ill to work. The doctor on site had no idea what was wrong and that night he nearly died of pneumonia and the purge.

---

13 July 1926. William was sent to La Paz and spent the night with Dr Puig, the best doctor there. Next day he was put on a special train to Tacna on the coast but the doctors there could not help either, however the Royal Mail ship was passing and William saw the ship's doctor who gave his opinion. It was a much better climate in Tacna but William's health did not improve sufficiently to return to work. Money ran out so finally he booked a passage home on MV *Lagunas*.

It was a very rough voyage and on arrival in England he was sent to a nursing home for two weeks after which his money again ran out, so he went to his parents' flat and after a fortnight commenced short walks.

The doctor advised not doing any work for some time and not to return to the high altitudes of Bolivia for at least a year. To use the time usefully he went to the Camborne School of Mines from January to June 1927 where he gained a first-class certificate dated August 1927, and on 28 September 1927 he signed a contract with the Bisichi Tin Company (Nigeria).